R. D. Mussey M. D.
with best regards of
Saml Batchelder

INTRODUCTION

AND

EARLY PROGRESS

OF THE

COTTON MANUFACTURE

IN THE

UNITED STATES.

"How strange it is that so few attempts have been made to trace the rise and progress of this great branch of industry, the Cotton Manufacture; to mark the successive steps of its advancement, the solidity of the foundations on which it rests, and the influence which it has already had, and must continue to have, on the number and condition of the people." — McCulloch, *Edinburgh Review*.

BOSTON:
LITTLE, BROWN AND COMPANY,
1863.

RIVERSIDE, CAMBRIDGE:
PRINTED BY H. O. HOUGHTON.

PREFACE.

The Cotton Manufacture has attained such importance in the United States, as to excite an interest as to its early history. Many circumstances, apparently of little consequence at the time, depend at present on personal recollection, and unless placed upon record now, will, a few years hence, only be recognised in the uncertainty of tradition.

I propose therefore to bring together such particulars as I have collected from time to time to gratify my own curiosity, and to add such as can still be obtained from any reliable authorities, in relation to the introduction and progress of the Cotton Manufacture in this country; and some sketches of the state of the business in other countries, particularly in Great Britain, at the time when their cotton machinery was introduced here.

In pursuing my inquiries, besides the information received from many others, I have to acknowledge my particular obligations to Mr. Zachariah Allen of Providence, Mr. Edward E. Manton of the Manufacturers' Mutual Insurance Company, Boston, and to Col. Joshua Herrick, who at the age of about eighty years, is still actively engaged in the employment of the government, and able to communicate personally his recollections of the first Cotton Factory built in this country, at Beverly, Massachusetts.

It has been very difficult to obtain such information as I wished respecting matters of which there is no record, and in which no one has hitherto felt sufficient interest to transmit, in any available form, the facts within their knowledge; so that the following pages should only be considered an imperfect attempt to preserve such fragments as may be useful to some one, who may in future be able to treat the subject more satisfactorily.

SAMUEL BATCHELDER.

Cambridge, October, 1863.

COTTON MANUFACTURE IN THE UNITED STATES.

When our attention is called to the history of the Cotton Manufacture, we cannot fail to be struck with the change that has taken place, both in this country and in Europe, during the life of a single generation. Nor is this change confined to those actually employed in the business, but extends to the habits, occupation, and condition of a great proportion of the population.

It was only by reason of a fortunate concurrence of several improvements in labor-saving machinery that such an extension of the cultivation and manufacture of cotton was rendered possible.

Without the application of rollers to the drawing of the thread, and the consequent use of water-power in spinning, the whole population of Great Britain, exclusive of those employed in agriculture, would not be able to produce the quantity of yarn now spun in that country; and without the application of steam-power, all the waterfalls in the island would be insufficient to drive the machinery.

Without the invention of Whitney's cotton-gin it would have been impossible for this country to have supplied the raw material for the increasing wants of the manufacturer; — and when by these means the production of cotton yarn had exceeded the ability of the hand-loom weaver, to convert it into cloth, the invention of the power-loom not only supplied the deficiency, but gave a new impulse to all the preliminary branches of the manufacture.

It is thus that mutual wants concur to stimulate improvements; and the introduction of cotton machinery—which in England was opposed by mobs and violence on account of an apprehension that laborers would be thrown out of employment, and in this country was regarded with little favor, from the fear that the female part of the population, by the disuse of the distaff, should become idle—has resulted in the profitable employment of a much larger number than could have been supported by the business in the former laborious process, without the aid of machinery, and, besides, has reduced the cost of cotton clothing to a degree which adds much to the comfort and probably also to the average duration of human life.

In speaking of the cotton manufacture, I wish to be understood as indicating such operations as are carried on by the use of machinery driven by water or steam power, or by other means than the direct application of human labor. The introduction of such machinery marks a great era in the world's history, not simply in relation to those directly employed in the business, but also by the market afforded, and the encouragement given for raising such quantities of the raw material as the whole population of the world would scarcely be able to spin and weave, by the use of the single spindle and the hand-shuttle.

Until about forty years previous to the commencement of our Revolutionary War, all the fabrics made of cotton were woven on the common loom, in which the shuttle was thrown through the web with one hand, and caught with the other, and this operation repeated for every thread of the woof. The yarn was spun upon a wheel with a single spindle, and the cotton was prepared for spinning by the laborious operation of carding with a pair of hand-cards.

Stock cards were substituted for hand cards

at a date which cannot be well ascertained, and in 1748, August 30th, a patent was granted to Lewis Paul, in which he describes the use of a card cylinder operating upon cards placed beneath. Further improvements in carding were said to have been made by Lees and Hargraves, but there is no record of any patent to either.

About this time many attempts were made to apply machinery to the spinning of cotton. Among the first which went into operation with any success was the Spinning Jenny, which was little else than uniting a number of spindles in the same machine, but operating by extending and twisting the thread in the same manner as on the one-thread wheel by hand.

During the period from 1768 to 1775, Arkwright obtained his patents for spinning by means of rollers, and for machinery for the carding and preparation of the cotton in a manner adapted to that mode of spinning. These were the great points in the establishment of manufacturing by machinery. The other branches of the business had in the mean time become so far perfected, that, in 1774, an Act of Parliament was passed to prevent the exportation of cotton machinery, with the intention of confining those improvements to Great Britain, and thus securing a monopoly of this branch of manufacturing.

During our Revolutionary War, Arkwright was improving and extending the manufacture of cotton. His patents were contested, and sometimes his machinery was broken by mobs; and in 1781, by a failure in one of his suits in the Court of King's Bench, the use of his machinery became public, and his patents were finally declared void in 1785.

In 1782 Watt took his patent for the steam-engine; and in 1785 cylinder printing was invented by Bell. So that the close of our Revolutionary War found England in possession of all the elements of her great manufacturing prosperity, and prepared to extend the business as fast as a supply of raw material could be furnished.

At this time, 1784, the quantity of cotton used in England annually was supposed to be only about 11,000,000 pounds.*

In the correspondence of the Earl of Chatham, Vol. II. p. 420, it is stated in a note that, "in 1766, cotton, as an article of commerce, was scarcely known in Great Britain. The entire value of cotton goods manufac-

* In *The Cotton Trade of Great Britain*, by Mann, pp. 93, 94, the quantity of cotton consumed in 1781 is stated at 5,101,990 pounds, and in 1859 at 976,600,000 pounds.

tured at the accession of George the Third being estimated to amount to only £200,000 sterling a year; and in 1782 the whole produce of the cotton manufacture did not exceed £2,000,000." In 1859 the exports alone were above £48,000,000.

Pepys, in his Diary, under date of Feb. 27, 1664, says: "Sir Martin Noel told us, the dispute between him, as farmer of the additional duty, and the East India Company, whether calico be *linen* or no, which he says it is, having been ever returned so. They say it is made of *cotton wool* and *grows upon trees*."

The printed calicoes made in Great Britain before the time of Arkwright's inventions were always made with linen warp, the cotton spun by hand not being strong enough for that purpose.

When by means of Arkwright's machinery cotton yarn was made suitable for warps, the prejudice against new inventions was such that the manufacturers could not be prevailed upon to weave it into calicoes. Mr. Strutt was at length successful in weaving a considerable quantity, when it was discovered that they were subject to double the duty of those manufactured with linen warp, and, when printed, were prohibited. He had therefore to petition Parliament for relief, which was obtained, after much opposition from the Lancashire manufacturers.

About this time, 1781, the English began to import some cotton from Brazil, and ten years later from the United States; but the quantity proved altogether inadequate to supply the demands of the increasing manufactures of England, on account of the difficulty of separating the cotton from the seed, either by the hand or any machinery then in use, particularly of the kind which was best adapted to cultivation in our soil and climate. At this time, 1793, the invention of the saw-gin by Eli Whitney removed the difficulty.

Thus step by step, in Great Britain and this country, within little more than half a century, improvements have been made in the manufacture and production of cotton, which have given it great importance in finance and political economy, and no small influence in international affairs.

The attention of Hamilton was drawn at a very early period to the importance of the cultivation and manufacture of cotton. The following extracts are from two pamphlets published by him in 1774 and 1775, in vindication of the measures of Congress.

"With respect to cotton, you do not pretend to deny that a sufficient quantity may be produced. Several of the Southern colonies are so favorable to it that, with due cultivation, in a couple of years they would afford enough to clothe the whole continent. As to the expense of bringing it by land, the best way will be to manufacture it where it grows, and afterwards transport it to the other colonies. Upon this plan I apprehend the expense would not be greater than to build and equip large ships to import the manufactures of Great Britain from thence. If we were to turn our attention from external to internal commerce, we would give greater facility and more lasting prosperity to our country than she can possibly have otherwise. . . . . . . If by the necessity of the thing manufactures should once be established and take root among us, they will pave the way still more to the future grandeur and glory of America." *Life of Hamilton,* by his son, Vol. I. pp. 29–35.

The foregoing extracts show a remarkable anticipation and foreshadowing of coming events in regard both to the cultivation and manufacture of cotton, at a time when there was little promise or anticipation of either, and indicate a wonderful maturity of judgment in a youth of eighteen.

The first attempt at manufacturing cotton by machinery in England, of which we have any account, was the invention, by John Wyatt, of Litchfield, of machinery for spinning, for which a patent was taken in 1738 in the name of Lewis Paul.*

A mill was built at Birmingham in 1741 or 1742, which was turned by two asses walking round an axis; and ten girls were employed in attending the work. This establishment was unsuccessful, and the machinery was sold in 1743.

A work upon a larger scale upon a stream of water was established at Northampton, with 250 spindles, and employed fifty hands; but the work did not prosper, and in 1764 passed into other hands, as appears from the letter of Charles Wyatt, the son of the inventor, published in Baines's History of the Cotton Manufacture, p. 135.

In 1733, John Kay of Colchester invented the fly-shuttle, which was used by the woollen weavers, whose cloth was usually so wide as to require one person on each side of the loom to throw the shuttle; but it was used very little by weavers of cotton until 1760, when his son, Robert Kay, invented the drop-box, by means of which the weaver can use

* See note A. at end of volume.

any one of three shuttles, with weft of different colors, at pleasure.*

About 1740, manufacturing was commenced at Manchester. The merchants supplied the weavers with warps, which were of linen yarn imported from Germany, and with raw cotton for the weft, which the weavers employed their own families, or other parties, to card and spin.

At this time the carding was done by hand-cards,—the spinning on the common one-thread wheel, and the weaving on the hand-loom.

To facilitate the supply of weft for the weavers, which it was difficult to procure in sufficient quantity, the spinning-jenny was invented by Thomas Highs, about 1764. He also claims the invention of spinning by rollers, having made some experiments with rollers before they were used by Arkwright.

About this time various improvements were made in the carding machinery to supersede the hand-cards then in use, which resulted in the introduction of a cylinder card, from which the cotton was taken by hand.

* In the patent of John Kay, May 26, 1833, the specification in describing the operation of the fly-shuttle says: "The weaver sits in the middle of the loom and pulls a small cord, which casts the shuttle from side to side at pleasure. The cloth is more even than it is where the layer (lay) is pulled by two men, one at each end of the loom."

In 1772, John Lees invented the feeder, and James Hargreaves, who had made important improvements in the spinning-jenny, was said to have invented the crank and comb for taking the cotton from the card; and Thomas Wood, in 1774, obtained what was called a perpetual or endless carding, by nailing the cards on the cylinder spirally instead of longitudinally,—for which he obtained a patent in 1776. All of these improvements were combined in Arkwright's machinery; for which he took his second patent in 1775; and the parties above named claimed one or another of these inventions; and Guest, in his "History of the Cotton Manufacture," seems to admit all these claims in his anxiety to limit the merit of Arkwright, and says he used a revolving can for twisting the rovings, or perpetual carding, which had been used for that purpose by Butler as early as 1759, which was before any machinery for producing such roving or perpetual carding was invented.

It is not always easy to decide to whom we ought to award the merit of many inventions, which may have been the study of various ingenious mechanics for years without success; and it happens in relation to cotton machinery, as in other mechanical inventions, that there are conflicting claims to all the most important improvements, after they are put in operation. Many may have been engaged for a long time in unsuccessful attempts to accomplish the object, and among them some who have been partially successful, but not so far as to make their schemes of any practical utility. At length some one with better advantages, or better workmanship, or by the application of the same principles with more skill and better judgment, builds a machine which goes into successful operation. In such a case all the unsuccessful schemers rise up and say, "I tried that principle," or "I put that wheel in operation years ago"; and thus all those, who condemn themselves by having made the attempt without success, come before the public and contend for the merit of the more fortunate or more skilful mechanic who has brought the plan to perfection.

Something of this kind probably occurred in relation to the invention of Arkwright's spinning machinery. According to the evidence on the trial in relation to his patent in 1785, it would appear that Highs, who invented the spinning-jenny in 1763 or 1764, afterward made some experiments or attempts at spinning with rollers, but without succeeding so far as to make it of any practical use. It seems probable that Arkwright became acquainted with the experiments of Highs, and was able, by combination with his own plans, to mature the invention, and put it in successful operation. This, as well as most other important improvements, is the result of successive experiments and failures, — until some one who becomes acquainted with the unsuccessful schemes, and has the skill and good judgment to remedy the defects, succeeds in perfecting the invention.

In 1780 there were twenty water-frame factories, the property of Mr. Arkwright, or of parties who had paid him for permission to use his machinery; and after his patent was made public in 1785, the number increased so rapidly that in 1790 there were one hundred and fifty cotton factories in England and Wales.

Soon after the renewal of intercourse, which took place between this country and Great Britain in consequence of the peace of 1783, we obtained some knowledge that during the war and the contest with us for the few years preceding, she had commenced a new branch of business, which she was pursuing and extending with wonderful success; but in consequence of their laws, passed in 1774, against the exportation of machinery and the emigration of mechanics and manufacturers, our information on the subject was for a long time confined to vague and uncertain rumor.

Tench Coxe says, in his Report in 1810: "In 1786 I became acquainted with the fact that labor-saving spinning machinery was considerable in Great Britain. It was understood that it was applicable at that time only to the carding and spinning of cotton, which we then constantly imported from foreign countries, apparently to the amount of our whole consumption. In the course of the following autumn and winter, repeated examinations and considerations of the subject occasioned very high expectations from a few well authenticated facts in relation to the production of the cotton raw material in gardens and other small pieces of land as far north as 38° 45′, — the County of Talbot, Maryland, and in some other places on the rivers of the Chesapeake Bay. It was inferred, that, as the shrub or the tree grew in that central degree of our country, all the extensive region south of 39° was capable of producing cotton, which is found in climates not only hotter than those of North America, but in the torrid zone. It was therefore confidently presumed that the cotton-spinning mill might be brought into very beneficial use in the United States. The production of cotton in the old settlements of Virginia was carefully examined as a test of this opinion, and opportunities offered to make it in a manner commanding entire confidence.

"After the more exact information of the existence and operation of the labor-saving machinery in Europe had led to due reflection on the incalculable importance of the vast capacity of this country to produce the proper raw material, the effectual measures were actively pursued to excite the attention of the whole community, and particularly of the planters of the five original Southern States. But, though our capacity to produce the cotton was so great, as at this time we know it to have always been,—though labor-saving machinery was effecting a gainful revolution in manufactures in Great Britain,—though cotton was then worth in the United States forty-four cents per pound, owing to foreign trade-laws,—and though it was at high prices in many parts of Europe,—several years had elapsed before sufficient attention to the culture could be excited, even by the numerous publications which were incessantly made."

In addition to the foregoing from Tench

Coxe, I make the following extract from a pamphlet by Dr. G. Emerson of Philadelphia, entitled "Cotton in the Middle States," published last year (1862): —

"Long before the Southern States took up its regular culture, cotton was raised on the eastern shore of Maryland, lower counties of Delaware, and other places in the Middle States. As early as 1736, and for some time after, it was chiefly regarded as an ornamental plant, and confined to gardens; but it soon became appreciated for its useful qualities, and was brought under regular cultivation. This culture, though comparatively limited in those places, has never been entirely abandoned up to the present day. I have myself seen many families who came from Sussex County, Delaware, to reside in the adjoining County of Kent, wearing clothes made of cotton of their own raising, spinning, and weaving.

"The culture of cotton in this section of our country gradually diminished in consequence of the vast area over which the plant was extended in more southern States. In competition with these, our more northern farmers found they possessed superior advantages for raising other field-crops, from which they derived greater profits.

"Limited as has been the culture of cotton on the peninsula between the Delaware and Chesapeake Bays, it has furnished a demonstration of the highest importance to our country. In proof of this it may be stated, that, at the close of the Revolution, a convention was held at Annapolis, in 1786, to consider what means could be best resorted to for the purpose of remedying the embarrassment of the country, then so much exhausted in its finances. The late President Madison, a member of this convention, from Virginia, there expressed it as his opinion, *that, from the results of cotton raising in Talbot County, Maryland, and numerous other proofs furnished in Virginia, there was no reason to doubt 'that the United States would one day become a great cotton-producing country!'*

"It would hence appear that the first culture of cotton in the United States, worthy of notice, was made on the peninsula between the Delaware and Chesapeake Bays, from whence it crossed into Western Maryland and Virginia, and so went southwards."

Dr. Emerson further reports that cotton has heretofore been raised in the lower portion of the peninsula between the Delaware and Chesapeake Bays, so as to form an important item in home industry. A colored family came last year from Sussex County to live in Camden, Delaware, bringing with them the seed of cotton, which they had continued to cultivate, and spin and weave for clothing. The cotton in this new situation perfected itself well, as appears from a boll in my possession; and Dr. Emerson proposes to plant several acres with this seed, which had become acclimated, so that, according to the experience of the last season, the cotton matured much more perfectly in that location from seed that had been raised there than from seed procured at distant places.

In relation to the first cultivation of cotton in Carolina and Georgia, the following are extracts from a letter given by Tench Coxe from Richard Teake, dated Savannah, Dec. 11, 1788: "I have been this year an adventurer, and the first that has attempted on a large scale in the article of cotton. Several here, as well as in Carolina, have followed me, and tried the experiment. . . . . I shall raise about five thousand pounds in the seed from about eight acres of land, and next year I expect to plant from fifty to one hundred acres. . . . . . The lands in the southern part of this State are admirably adapted to the raising of this commodity. The climate is so mild so far to the South, scarce any winter is felt, and — another grand advantage — *whites can be employed.* The labor is not severe attending it, not more than raising Indian corn."

In relation to the origin of Sea Island cotton, he gives, as communicated by Dr. Mease, a letter from Patrick Walsh, from which the following is extracted: "It is pleasing to view the rising prosperity of the land you live in, and particularly so, too, when I reflect that one of the present sources of her riches was, in a very great measure, derived from myself. In the year 1785 I settled in Kingston, Jamaica, where, finding my friend Frank Leavet, with his family and all his negroes, in a distressed situation, he applied to me for advice as to what steps he should take, having no employment for his slaves. I advised him to go to Georgia and settle on some of the islands, and plant provisions until something better turned up. . . . . At length he resolved to go to the place I recommended. Early in the year 1786 I sent him a large quantity of various seeds of Jamaica; and Mr. Moss and Colonel Brown requested me to get some of the Pernambuco cotton seed, of which I sent him three large sacks, of which he made no use but by accident. In a letter to me in 1789 he said: 'Being in want of the sacks for gathering in my provisions, I shook their contents on the dung-hill, and it happening to be a very wet season, in the spring multitudes of plants covered the place. These I drew out and transplanted them into two acres of ground, and was highly gratified to find an abundant crop. This encouraged me to plant more. I used all my strength in cleaning and planting, and have succeeded beyond my most sanguine expectations.'"

In 1789, South Carolina and Georgia were at a very low ebb. Their great staples, rice and indigo, had declined in price, and they had not as yet entered on the cultivation of cotton. Ædanus Burke, in a debate on the tariff, on the 16th of April, 1789, to induce the House to lay a considerable duty on hemp and cotton, gave a melancholy picture of the situation of those States. "The staple products of South Carolina and Georgia," he observed, "were hardly worth cultivation on account of their fall in price. The lands were certainly well adapted to the growth of hemp, and he had no doubt but its culture would be practised with attention. Cotton was likewise in contemplation among them, and if good seed could be procured, he hoped might succeed."

Considering that among the complaints against Great Britain before the Revolution some of the principal were the restrictions upon trade and intercourse between the colonies, and the discouragement, and prohibition in many cases, of manufacturing for themselves, it is not surprising to find that, at the close of the war, we very soon turned our attention to the introduction of such branches of manufacture as promised any advantage; and the recent improvements that had been made in the application of machinery to the manufacture of cotton in Great Britain could not fail to make this a prominent object. Accordingly we find, that, as early as 1786, before the adoption of the Constitution of the United States, the Legislature of Massachusetts was offering an encouragement for the introduction of machinery for carding and spinning cotton.

On the 25th of October, 1786, Richard Cranch of the Senate, and Mr. Clarke and Mr. Bowdoin of the House, were appointed — "to view any new invented machines that are making within this Commonwealth for the purpose of manufacturing sheep's and cotton wool, and report what measures are proper for the Legislature to take to encourage the same." This committee reported that "they had examined those very curious and useful machines made by Robert and Alexander Barr for the purpose of carding and spinning cotton." And, in accordance with the further report of the committee, a resolve was passed on the 16th of November, 1786, granting the sum of £200, "to enable them to complete the said three machines, and also a roping machine, and to construct such other machines as are necessary for the purpose of carding, roping, and spinning of sheep's wool, as well as of cotton wool."

On the 8th of March, 1787, "Richard Cranch was appointed by the Senate, with such as the House should join, to examine the machines, which are now nearly completed,"—and to examine and allow the account of Robert and Alexander Barr; "and also to report to the next General Court what gratuity in their opinion the said Robert and Alexander justly deserve, as a reward for their ingenuity in forming those machines, and as an encouragement for their public spirit in making them known to this Commonwealth."

The committee allow their account to the amount of £189 12*s.*, in which is contained an item for "expense in transporting the machines to and from Boston,"—from which we may infer that they were exhibited to the Legislature.

On May 2, 1787, a resolve was passed discharging them from the £200, and granting them *six tickets* in the land lottery;—and providing further, that said machines should be left under the care of Hugh Orr, Esq., who is "requested to explain to such citizens as may apply for the same the principles on which said machines are constructed and the advantages arising from their use, both by verbal explanations, and by letting them see the machinery at work."

According to Judge Mitchell's "History of Bridgewater," Colonel Hugh Orr of that place was instrumental in the first introduction of cotton machinery into this country. Hugh Orr was born at Lochwinnock in Scotland, January 2, 1715, and came to America June 17, 1740, and settled at Bridgewater, where he died December 6, 1798. He was engaged there before the Revolution in the manufacture of fire-arms, and at the commencement of that war made the first cannon that were made in this country by boring from the solid casting. He is said to have invited Robert and Alexander Barr, brothers, from Scotland, in order to construct at his works in East Bridgewater machinery for carding, roving, and spinning cotton.

Thomas Somers, another Scotchman, under

the direction of Mr. Orr, constructed other machinery for the same purpose; and on the eighth of March, 1787, the General Court placed in the hands of Mr. Orr twenty pounds for the encouragement of the artist. Mr. Orr also, about the same time, employed another foreigner, by the name of McClure, to weave *jeans* and *corduroys* by hand with the fly-shuttle.

In March, 1787, a petition was before the Legislature of Massachusetts, from Thomas Somers, said to have been a midshipman in the English navy, representing, "that, in the fall of the year 1785, the tradesmen and manufacturers of Baltimore, having formed themselves into an association in order to apply to the Legislature in behalf of American manufactures, being stimulated thereto by a circular letter received from a committee of the tradesmen and manufacturers of the town of Boston. Your petitioner, then residing in Baltimore (having been formerly brought up to the cotton manufactory, and willing to contribute what lay in his power to introduce said manufacture in America), did, at his own risk and expense, go to England in order to prepare the machines for carding and spinning cotton. That, after much difficulty, your petitioner found that he could only take descriptions and models of said engines; with which he returned to Baltimore last summer. Soon after his arrival he found they were very dilatory about encouraging the matter, and with the advice of some friends he resolved to try what might be done in Boston."

On this petition,—"with a view to encourage the aforesaid manufacture, and to give the said Somers an opportunity to give specimens of his abilities to perfect the manufactures set forth in his said petition,—*Resolved*, that there be paid out of the public treasury, by warrant from the governor and council, twenty pounds, lawful money, to be applied to the purposes aforesaid, which sum shall be deposited in the hands of Hugh Orr, Esq., of Bridgewater, who shall be a committee to superintend the application of the same."

Passed March 8, 1787.

By these proceedings it appears, that, in 1786 and 1787, the Legislature of Massachusetts were taking active measures to encourage the introduction of cotton machinery, and that they had succeeded in obtaining machines and models, probably including the roller-spinning and other improvements of Arkwright, which had then been but partially introduced in England, after the failure of his suit for establishing his rights against Colonel Mordaunt in 1781.—Another action, having been tried in 1785, resulted in his favor; but that decision was soon reversed, so that his machinery was freely used within a few years of that time.

It does not appear that the machinery at East Bridgewater was used to any extent for manufacturing purposes, but rather for models and to diffuse information upon the subject; and the Legislature had provided in their resolve, — "that public notice be given for three weeks successively in Adam's and Nurse's newspaper, that said machines may be seen and examined at the house of the Hon. Hugh Orr in Bridgewater, and that the manner of working them will be explained."

There is no doubt that the machinery at Bridgewater was the first built or introduced into this country for the manufacture of cotton, which included Arkwright's roller-spinning and other patent improvements.

A factory was commenced at Beverly, in 1787, expressly for the manufacture of cotton goods, with such machinery as could then be procured; and finding the construction of the machinery very difficult and expensive, and the prospects very discouraging, they made application to the Legislature for aid, which in February, 1789, passed the following

"Resolve for encouraging the Cotton Manufactory at Beverly, — Feb. 17, 1789.

"Whereas it is essential to the true interests of this Commonwealth to encourage within the same the introduction and establishment of such manufactures as will give the most extensive and profitable employment to its citizens, and thereby, instead of those emigrations which are ruinous to the State, increase the number of manufacturers, who by consuming the productions of the soil will add to the value of it; and Whereas, John Cabot and others, who have been incorporated by the name of 'The Proprietors of the Beverly Cotton Manufactory,' have set forth to this Court the difficulties and extraordinary expenses that attend the introduction of the Cotton Manufactory to be such as require the assistance of Government: For the support and encouragement of said manufactory; *Be it Resolved,*—That there be granted, and there hereby is granted accordingly, and conveyed to John Cabot, Joshua Fisher, Henry Higginson, Moses Brown, George Cabot, Andrew Cabot, Israel Thorndike, Isaac Chapman, and Deborah Cabot, they being members of the said corporation, the value of Five hundred pounds, lawful money in specie, to be paid in the Eastern lands, the property of this Commonwealth;—the said lands to be valued, ascertained and conveyed by the Committee for the sale thereof;—to have and to hold the same, with the appurtenances, to them and their heirs and assigns forever, for their use as tenants in common in the proportion following, to wit: to the said John Cabot ten fortieth parts; to the said Joshua Fisher nine fortieth parts; to the said Henry Higginson four fortieth parts; to the said Moses Brown four fortieth parts; to the said George Cabot four fortieth parts; to the said Andrew Cabot two fortieth parts; to the said Israel Thorndike four fortieth parts; to the said Isaac Chapman one fortieth part; and to the said Deborah Cabot two fortieth parts. Provided, however, that this resolve and the grant aforesaid shall be void, and the said land shall again revert to this Commonwealth, unless the said corporation or the said grantees, their heirs or assigns, shall manufacture, within seven years from the passage of this Resolve, a quantity of cotton and linen piece-goods, of a quality usually imported into this Commonwealth, not less than fifty thousand of yards; and shall keep in a book a full and true account of the several kinds and the quantity of each kind, and the value of the same, which account shall be verified by the testimony of at least two of the proprietors, on oath, and a fair copy thereof be lodged in the Secretary's office; — or unless the said corporation or the said grantees, their heirs or assigns, shall pay to the treasurer of this Commonwealth five hundred pounds in gold or silver, within eight years after the passing of this Resolve."

At the same session of the Legislature an Act was passed to incorporate the "Beverly Manufacturing Company," authorized to hold personal property to the amount of £80,000, and real estate to the amount of £10,000, the same parties being named in the Act of incorporation as in the Resolve above quoted, and also including the name of Thomas Somers, who had petitioned the Legislature in 1787 for aid in building cotton machinery from the designs he had brought from England.

Besides the usual provisions in Acts of incorporation, that for incorporating the Beverly Cotton Manufactory contained the following: "That all goods, which may be manufactured by said corporation, shall have a label of lead affixed to one end thereof, which shall have the same impression with the seal of the said corporation; and that if any person shall knowingly use a like seal or label, with that used by said corporation, by annexing the same to any cotton, or cotton and linen goods not manufactured by said corporation, with a view of vending or disposing thereof as the proper manufactures of the said corporation, every person so offending shall forfeit and pay treble the value of such goods, to be sued for and recovered for the use of said corporation by action of debt in any court of record proper to try the same."

It appears that the proprietors had not found the grant of land, before recited, available for their purpose, and that in June, 1790, a petition was presented to the Legislature in their behalf, signed by John Cabot and Joshua Fisher, managers. They represent —

"That they had expended about four thousand pounds, and that the present value of their stock was not equal to two thousand, and that a farther very considerable advancement is absolutely necessary; that the intended aid by a grant of land made by a former legislature has not, in any degree, answered the purpose of it, and pray that in lieu of that grant some real and ready assistance may be afforded them."

The petitioners state, as one of the public advantages to be derived from the manufacture of cotton, that the raw material is procured (from the West Indies) in exchange for fish, "the most valuable export in possession of the State." They mention the extraordinary cost of machines, intricate and difficult in their construction, without any model in the country, and instance a carding-machine that cost eleven hundred dollars.

The petition was referred to a committee, of which Nathaniel Gorham was chairman, who reported, "that the petitioners have a grant of one thousand pounds, to be raised in a lottery, on condition that they give bonds that the money be actually appropriated in such a way as will most effectually promote the manufacturing of cotton piece-goods in this Commonwealth."

This factory at Beverly was in operation at the time of Washington's visit to the North in 1789, as appears by the following extract from his Diary: "Friday, 30th October.—A little after eight o'clock I set out (from Salem) for Newburyport, and in less than two miles crossed the bridge between Salem and Beverly, which makes a handsome appearance, and is upon the same plan of those over Charles and Mystic rivers, excepting that it has not footways, as that of the former has. The length of the bridge is 1530 feet, and was built for about £4500 lawful money,—a price inconceivably low in my estimation, as there is eighteen feet water in the deepest parts of the river, over which it is erected. The bridge is longer than that at Charlestown, but shorter by —— feet than the other over Mystic. All of them have drawbridges by which vessels pass. After passing Beverly two miles, we come to a cotton manufactory, which seems to be carrying on with spirit by the Cabots (principally). In this manufactory they have the new invented Carding and Spinning machines. One of the first supplies the work, and four of the latter, one of which spins 84 threads at a time by one person. The cotton is prepared for these machines by being first (lightly) drawn to a thread, on the common wheel. There is also another machine for doubling and twisting the threads for particular cloths; this also does many at a time. For winding the cotton from the spindles and preparing it for the warp, there is a reel, which expedites the work greatly. A number of looms (15 or 16) were at work with spring shuttles, which do more than double work. In short, the whole seemed perfect, and the cotton stuffs which they turn out excellent of their kind; — warp and filling both cotton."

Extract from Washington's Diary, — an edition of which was privately printed, 1858, for Wm. J. Davis, New York.

This factory was built of brick, and was continued in operation to some extent for several years. It was driven by *horse-power;* and a gentleman is still living, who was, a few years ago, a member of Congress, and is yet an active octogenarian in government employ, and who remembers, when a boy, occasionally driving a pair of large bay horses to give motion to the wheels.

I have been thus particular in regard to the mill at Beverly, because it was the earliest enterprise undertaken and carried into execution in this country for manufacturing cotton, and was certainly in operation some time before 1789, though Governor Woodbury, who was of a Beverly family, says, in his famous report upon Cotton, — *the first cotton factory built in the United States was at Providence in* 1790.

Mr. Samuel Witherill of Philadelphia was engaged at a very early period in commencing various manufacturing operations. An address was delivered by Tench Coxe to an assembly of the friends of American manufactures, convened for the purpose of establishing a *Society for the Encouragement of the Useful Arts*, August 9, 1787. The extent and success of the operations of this society for the first year may be seen by the report of the managers in August, 1788, signed by Samuel Witherill, Jr., Chairman, — in which it is stated that the amount of cash received from the contributors on the 23d of August was £1327 10s. 6d.; that they had purchased a quantity of flax, and employed between two and three hundred women in spinning linen yarn, and also engaged workmen to make a carding-engine, and four jennies, of forty, forty-four, sixty, and eighty spindles, for spinning cotton; that, as soon as the season would permit the house to be fitted up, they were set to work, but, owing to various delays and obstructions thrown in their way *by foreign agents*, it was the 12th of April, 1788, before they began to weave, and on the 23d of August, 1788, they had made 11,367 yards of various kinds of linen and cotton goods.

In 1790 a person, who had been employed in the Beverly factory, was engaged to go to Norwich, Connecticut, to put in operation some cotton machinery, which was understood to be similar to that used at Beverly. This machinery was not built in this country, but was supposed to have been imported, by some means, from England. The parties engaged in the business at Norwich were Mr. Huntington, Dr. Lathrop, and others. This Dr. Lathrop was the same in whose druggist's shop Benedict Arnold is said to have been employed, before the Revolutionary War.—See *Sparks's American Biography*, Vol. III.

Another cotton mill in Connecticut was built in the west part of New Haven, in 1794, by John R. Livingston and David Dickson, of New York. Previous to this time they had a small mill not far from Hurlgate, on the New York side; — the machinery was moved to New Haven, and was in full operation in 1795. In 1807 this was converted into a woollen-mill, and since into a paper-mill.

In 1806 General Humphrey built his mill at Derby (since Humphreysville), both for cotton and woollen.

William Pollard of Philadelphia obtained a patent for cotton-spinning, Dec. 30, 1791, which was the first water-frame put in motion in Pennsylvania. Whether he obtained his patterns direct from England, or by the way of Providence, is not certain, or whether the machinery was capable of being put in successful operation may be doubtful, for the business failed at a time when the machinery of Slater was producing great profits. It was, however, an early attempt at the introduction of water-spinning in that part of the country, and its want of success probably retarded the progress of cotton-spinning in Philadelphia. Some accounts say the mill was burned.

In 1808 the Globe factory, with a capital of $80,000, was established under Dr. Redman Coxe, of Philadelphia.

The Arkwright machinery was introduced very early, at Copp's Creek, Delaware, by Goodfellow; also at Kirkmill, near Wilmington.

A magnificent scheme was projected for a manufacturing establishment at Paterson, New Jersey, and a charter was obtained through the interest of Alexander Hamilton, granting, it is said, besides the usual powers of a manufacturing corporation, banking privileges, and the corporate powers of a city. A number of individuals from New York, New Jersey, and Pennsylvania had associated and raised a capital of about two hundred thousand dollars, and obtained extensive rights in the Great Falls of the Passaic. They were incorporated by the Legislature of New Jersey, November 22, 1791, by the name of "The Society for the Establishment of Useful Manufactures," and the Company was organized at New Brunswick during the same month. In May, 1792, they selected the site for their operations, and on the fourth of July made appropriations for building factories, machine shops, and print-works, and for the extensive use of water-power from the Passaic falls.

The construction of their canals was confided to Major L'Enfant,* a French engineer, whose gigantic schemes were far beyond the pecu-

* The same who was originally employed by Gen. Washington to survey and lay out the City of Washington, but who had some difficulty with the Commissioners before the business was finished. — *Sparks's Life of Washington*, Vol. X. p. 204.

niary means of the Company, so that in 1793 the business was put under the charge of Peter Colt, then Comptroller of the State of Connecticut, who completed the watercourses, and built a factory, in which they commenced spinning cotton yarn in 1794.

In the life of Samuel Slater a very particular account is given, by William Anthony, of the first attempts to introduce cotton machinery at Providence. He says: "About the year 1788 Daniel Anthony, Andrew Dexter, and Lewis Peck, all of Providence, entered into an agreement to make what was then called *homespun cloth.* The idea at first was to spin by hand, and make jeans with linen warp and cotton filling; but hearing that Mr. Orr of Bridgewater, Mass., had imported some models of machinery from England for the purpose of spinning cotton, it was agreed that Daniel Anthony should go to Bridgewater and get a draft of the model of said machine. He, in company with John Reynolds of East Greenwich, who had been doing something in the manufacturing of wool, went to Bridgewater and found the model of the machine spoken of in possession of Mr. Orr, but not in operation. It was not the intention of Mr. Orr to operate it, but he only kept it for the inspection of those who might have an inclination to take drafts."

This model of the machine was very imperfect, and was said to be taken from one of the first built in England. A draft of this machine was accordingly taken, and laid aside for a while. They then proceeded to build a machine of a different construction, called a jenny. I understood that a model of this machine was brought from England into Beverly, Massachusetts, by a man by the name of* Summers. This jenny had twenty-eight spindles, ... was finished in 1787.† It was first set up in a private house, and afterwards removed to the market-house chamber in Providence, and operated there.

Joshua Lindly of Providence was then engaged to build a carding-machine for carding the cotton, agreeably to the draft presented, obtained also from Beverly. This machine

* We here trace to Beverly the Thomas *Somers* who went to England from Baltimore, in 1785, for the purpose of procuring the English machinery, and to whom the grant of £20 was made by the Legislature of Massachusetts, March 8, 1787, to be expended under the direction of Mr. Orr.

† There must be a mistake in the *year*, as he says above that Dexter and others, for whom this machinery was built, entered into their agreement about 1788. This should be, in all probability, 1789, for the time when the jenny was finished. A further confirmation of this date is that Somers received from the Legislature of Massachusetts, March 8, 1787, a grant to enable him to complete his models; and it must have been after this time that he built the machines at Beverly from which those at Providence were designed.

was something similar to the one now used for carding wool, the cotton being taken off the machine in rolls, and roped by hand. After some delay this machine was finished. They then proceeded to build a spinning-frame after the draft obtained at Bridgewater. This machine was something similar to the water-frame now in use, but very imperfect. It consisted of eight heads of four spindles each, — being thirty-two spindles in all, — and was operated by a crank turned by hand. . . . . . The spinning-frame, after being tried some time in Providence, was carried to Pawtucket and attached to a wheel propelled by water. The work of turning the machine was too laborious to be done by hand, and the machine was too imperfect to be turned by water. Soon after this the machine was sold to Mr. Moses Brown of Providence; but as all the carding and roping was done by hand, it was very imperfect, and but little could be done.

This was the situation of cotton manufacturing in Rhode Island when Mr. Samuel Slater arrived in this country; — then all this imperfect machinery was thrown aside, and machinery more perfect built under his direction.

The spinning machinery described as building at Philadelphia was stated to be four spinning-jennies of forty, forty-four, sixty, and eighty spindles. That at Beverly is supposed to be of the same character, and that also which was put in operation at the market-house in Providence, which is described as a jenny with twenty-eight spindles, built after the model of that at Beverly, and which Mr. Anthony states to be on a different construction from the one at Bridgewater. So that in all these cases it is very evident that spinning by the jenny alone was attempted. But the spinning-machine built after the model of that in the possession of Mr. Orr, and built by Barr, appears to have been an attempt to introduce the Arkwright machinery. Mr. Anthony describes it as similar to the water-frame now in use; says it consisted of eight heads, of four spindles each; that it was operated by a crank, in neither of which particulars would it agree with the jenny, or any other spinning-machine known to have been in use; but the description, as far as it goes, would apply to the Arkwright spinning-frame, though he omits the great feature of Arkwright's spinning, the drawing or extension of the thread by means of rollers.

It is possible that Robert and Alexander Barr may have obtained such a knowledge of Arkwright's machinery after the failure of his suit in 1781, that they thought themselves able to construct his water-frame.

Samuel Slater at the age of twenty-one sailed from London on the 13th of September, 1789, and arrived at New York in November. He seems to have had a design of coming to America for some time, and what finally determined him was his observing in a Philadelphia paper a reward offered by a society for a machine to make *cotton rollers.** We see here, I suppose, the effect of an advertisement of the "Pennsylvania Society for promoting the *useful Arts*," mentioned above.

Soon after his arrival in New York, he wrote to Moses Brown as follows: —

"New York, December 2, 1789.

"Sir: A few days ago I was informed that you wanted a manager of cotton spinning, in which business I flatter myself that I can give the greatest satisfaction in making machinery, making as good yarn, either for stockings or twist, as any that is made in England, as I have had opportunity and an oversight of Sir Richard Arkwright's works, and in Mr. Strutt's mill upwards of eight years. If you are not provided for, should be glad to serve you;

* Probably this was intended to indicate a machine for *roller-spinning*.

though I am in the New York manufactory, and have been for three weeks, since I arrived from England. But we have only one card, two machines, two spinning-jennies, which I think are not worth using. My encouragement is pretty good, but should much rather have the care of *perpetual carding* and spinning. My intention is to erect a perpetual card and spinning (meaning the Arkwright patents). If you please to drop a line respecting the amount of encouragement you wish to give, by favor of Captain Brown, you will much oblige, sir,

"Your most obedient humble servant,

"SAMUEL SLATER.

"Please direct to me at No. 37 Golden Hill."

The reply of Mr. Brown is given as follows:—

"PROVIDENCE, 10 — 12th Month, 1781.

"FRIEND: I received thine of the 2d, and observe its contents. I, or rather Almy and Brown, who have the business in the cotton line, ... want the assistance of a person skilled in the frame- or water-spinning. An experiment has been made, which has failed, no person being acquainted with the business, and the frames imperfect. Thy being already engaged in a factory with many able proprietors, we can hardly expect we can give thee encouragement adequate to leaving thy present employ. As the frame we have is the first attempt of the kind that has been made in America, it is too imperfect to afford much encouragement. We hardly know what to say to thee, but if thou thought thou could'st perfect and conduct them to profit, if thou wilt come and do it, thou shalt have all the profits made of them, over and above the interest of the money they cost and the wear and tear of them. We will find stock and be repaid in yarn, as we may agree for six months, and this we do for the information thou canst give if fully acquainted with the business. . . . . . If thy present situation does not come up to what thou wishest, and from thy knowledge can be ascertained of the advantages of the mills so as to induce thee to come and work ours and have the *credit* as well as the advantage of perfecting the first water-mill in America, we should be glad to engage thy care, so long as they can be made profitable to both, and we can agree.

"I am, for myself and Almy & Brown,

"Thy friend,

"MOSES BROWN."

The following appears as an extract from a letter to Slater under the same date, which gives some particulars of the cotton machinery at Providence before the arrival of Slater. "We have two machines of this kind, one of thirty-two spindles, and one of twenty-four. They have been worked, and spun about one hundred and fifty skeins of cotton yarn, from five to eight skeins (of fifteen lays round a reel of two yards) to the pound. But the person we let the mill to being unacquainted with the business, and the mill probably not perfected, he could not make wages in attending them, and therefore they are at present still. We then wrought hand-roping, as the carding machine was not in order. We have since got a jenny, and are putting on fine cards to the machine. These, with one eighty-four and a sixty spinning-jenny, and a doubling and twisting jenny, compose the principal machinery about our factory."

In consequence of this correspondence, Slater soon left New York and came to Providence. A letter from Smith Wilkinson, "Life of Slater," p. 76, gives an account of his first visit to Pawtucket, and some particulars of the manufacturing business. He says: "Samuel Slater came to Pawtucket early in January 1790, in company with Moses Brown, William Almy, Obadiah Brown, and Smith Brown, who did a small business in Providence at manufacturing on billies and jennies driven by men, as were also the carding-machines. . . . There was a spinning-frame in the building, which used to stand on the southwest abutment of Pawtucket bridge, which was started for trial (after it was built for Andrew Dexter and Lewis Peck) by Joseph and Richard Anthony, but the machine was very imperfect and made very uneven yarn. The cotton for this experiment was carded by hand, and roped on a woollen wheel by a female."

"Mr. Slater entered into a contract with William Almy and Smith Brown, and commenced building a water-frame of twenty-four spindles, two carding-machines, and the drawing and roping frames necessary to prepare for the spinning, and soon after added a frame of forty-eight spindles. He commenced [spinning?] some time in the fall of 1790, or early in 1791. I was then in my tenth year, and went to work for him, and began at tending the breaker. The mode of laying the cotton was by the hand, taking up a handful and pulling it apart with both hands, and shifting it all into the right hand, to get the staple of the cotton straight, and fix the handful so as to hold it firm, and then applying it to the surface of the breaker, moving the hand horizontally across the card to and fro, until the cotton was fully prepared."

The description of this operation shows the rude state of the Arkwright machinery as introduced by Slater at that time.

A letter from Moses Brown of the 19th of April, 1791, addressed to Moses Brown of Beverly, "To be communicated to the proprietors of the Beverly factory," says: "I have for some time thought of addressing the Beverly manufacturers on the subject of an application to Congress for some encouragement to the cotton manufacture by an additional duty on the cotton goods imported, and the applying such duty as a bounty, partly for *raising and saving cotton in the Southern States, of a quality and cleanness suitable to be wrought by machines*,* and partly as a bounty on cotton goods of the kind manufactured in the United States; . . . . and it is the desire of those concerned this way, that you, being the first and largest, would take the lead, and devise such plan as may be most eligible to effect the purpose. Almy and Brown, who conduct the business of the cotton manufactory, with an English workman from Ark-

* When Slater first began to spin, he used Cayenne and Surinam cotton, but after a few years he began to mix about one third of Southern cotton; and this yarn was designated as second quality and sold at a price accordingly.

Hamilton, in his report on manufactures, says: "The extensive cultivation of cotton can perhaps hardly be expected, but from the previous establishment of domestic manufactories of the article."

wright's works, have completed the water spinning machines to the perfection to make the enclosed yarn,—the former mills, which I had purchased, made from the States model at Bridgewater, proving not to answer."

Another letter from Moses Brown, of October 15, 1791, addressed to John Dexter, gives an account of the early proceedings in Rhode Island in manufacturing, as follows: "In the spring of 1789, some persons in Providence had procured to be made a carding-machine, a jenny, and a spinning-frame to work by hand, after the manner of Arkwright's invention, taken principally from models belonging to the State of Massachusetts, which were made at their expense by two persons from Scotland, who took their ideas from observation and not from experience in the business. These machines, made here, not answering the purpose and expectation of the proprietors, and I being desirous of perfecting them, if possible, and the business of the cotton manufacture, so as to be useful to the country, I purchased them, and by great alterations the carding-machine and jenny were made to answer. The frames, with one other, on nearly the same construction, made from the same model, and tried without success at East Greenwich, which I also purchased, I attempted to set to work by water, and made a little yarn, so as to answer for warps; but being so imperfect, both as to quality and quantity of the yarn, their use was suspended until I could procure a person who had wrought or seen them wrought in Europe.

"Late in the fall I received a letter from a young man, then lately arrived at New York, from Arkwright's works in England, informing me of his situation, that he could hear of no perpetual spinning mills on the continent but mine, and proposed to come and work them. I wrote him, and he came accordingly; but on viewing the mills, he declined doing anything with them, and proposed making a new one, using such parts of the old as would answer." . .

He proceeds to say that they contracted with him "to direct and make a mill in his own way, which he did."

From the foregoing it appears very evident that all the first cotton machinery introduced at Beverly, Providence, Paterson, and Philadelphia, was confined to the spinning-jenny, and such improvements as had been introduced before the invention of Arkwright, and that the first Arkwright machinery was that built by Barr at Bridgewater, which was probably too imperfect to be put to any profitable use, so that to Slater justly belongs the credit of the successful introduction of the Arkwright machinery, and the establishment of the cotton manufacture in this country.

The second cotton mill built by Mr. Slater, called the "White Mill," was within the limits of Massachusetts, on the east side of Pawtucket River, in what was then the town of Rehoboth. At the session of the Massachusetts Legislature in June 1799, — "on the petition of Samuel Slater, stating his intention to establish a cotton mill in Rehoboth," — an Act was passed, providing "that all buildings that may be erected in said town for the purpose of a cotton mill, together with the materials and stock employed in the manufacture of cotton, be, and the same are hereby exempted from taxes of every kind, during the term of seven years from the first day of April next." (Passed June 22, 1799.) This was the first mill on the Arkwright system erected in Massachusetts, and must be the same referred to in the Life of Slater, where it is stated that in 1798 he entered into partnership with Oziel Wilkinson, Timothy Green, and William Wilkinson, and built a second mill on the east side of Pawtucket River;—and though the Act was passed in 1799, the building may have been in progress in 1798.

Until this time the business had been confined to Mr. Slater and his associates, but soon after this, it is stated that several of his men, who had become acquainted with the construction of his machinery, left his employment and commenced the erection of mills for themselves or other parties. Mr. Benj. S. Wolcott was employed by Mr. Slater in the construction of his first mill. After acquiring sufficient knowledge of the business, he united with Rufus and Elisha Waterman, for the purpose of erecting a cotton factory in Cumberland, about 1801. The machinery was afterwards removed to Central Falls, a short distance above Pawtucket, and a new company formed, with the addition of Mr. Stephen Jenks.

Another of his workmen by the name of Robbins commenced a mill in New Ipswich, which was put in operation in 1804, being the first cotton mill built in New Hampshire.

The "History of Rehoboth," which should be the best authority on the subject, says: "The first cotton factory that was erected upon the east side of the river in the village of Pawtucket was the 'Yellow Mill,' built in 1805." The first cotton mill on the east side of the river, and in Massachusetts, was that before mentioned in 1798, or 1799, — and the *second* mill was built there in 1805; for I find an Act passed by the Legislature of Massachusetts, June 14, 1805, providing "that all the buildings that are or may be erected in the town of Rehoboth by Eliphalet Slack, Oliver Starkweather, Eleaser Tyler, 2d, Elijah Ingraham, and others, for the purpose of establishing a cotton manufactory in said town, and all the materials and stock to be employed in the manufacture of cotton, be, and the same are hereby exempted from all taxes of every kind for and during the term of five years, from and after the passing of this Act."

In one of these early mills at Pawtucket, B. S. Wolcott, Jr. was employed, who with the assistance of his father, in 1807 or 1808, built the first cotton mill in Oneida County, New York, four miles west of Utica. Some years later, Mr. Wolcott, associated with Benj. and Joseph Marshall, formerly English merchants in New York, erected the "New York Mills." Mr. Gallatin, in his report on manufactures, April 17, 1810, is probably mistaken in saying "after the first cotton mill was erected in Rhode Island in 1791, another in the same State was built in 1795, and two more in the State of Massachusetts in 1803 and 1804." He may be more correct in what follows: "During the three succeeding years, ten were erected or commenced in Rhode Island, and one in Connecticut, making altogether fifteen mills erected before the year 1808, working at that time

8,000 spindles. Returns have been received of 87 mills, which were erected at the end of the year 1809, sixty-two of which were in operation, and worked 31,000 spindles, and the other twenty-five will be in operation in the course of the year 1810."

The first cotton mill in the vicinity of Boston, and the first in Massachusetts after that built by Slater at Rehoboth, was a small establishment on Bass River in Beverly, which was in operation in the fall of 1801, or early in 1802, with six water frames, of seventy-two spindles each. The machinery was built at Paterson, New Jersey, by a man of the name of Clark, who came to Beverly to put it in operation. The business was unsuccessful on account of the insufficiency of the water-power and other causes, and the mill continued in operation but two or three years. Thus it appears that Beverly, though never engaged in the cotton manufacture very extensively or with much profit, was the pioneer in the business, not only in building the first factory in 1787, but the first after Slater in extending the use of the Arkwright machinery in Massachusetts.

In 1806 John Slater, the brother of Samuel, had arrived from England, and united with Samuel and others in building, at Smithfield, the establishment now called Slatersville. He removed to this place in June 1806, and took charge of the concern; and in the spring of 1807 the works were sufficiently advanced to commence spinning.

In 1807, Mr. Zachariah Allen estimated the whole number of spindles in operation in the United States at about four thousand.

By this time the manufacturing of cotton was extending itself, and factories were built in many of the towns near Providence, both in Massachusetts and Rhode Island, so that in 1809, according to Benedict's "History of Rhode Island," there were seventeen cotton mills in operation within the *town* of Providence and its vicinity, working 14,296 spindles, and at the commencement of the war with Great Britain, in 1812, there were said to be, within thirty miles of Providence in the State of

Rhode Island,	33	factories,		30,660	spindles,
Massachusetts,	20	"		17,370	"
making	53	"	with	48,030	"

The statistics of Tench Coxe, from the census of 1810, give for the State of Rhode Island —

Cotton factories, 28; spindles, 21,178.

According to an account taken by John H. Pitman, of Providence, there were in the State of Rhode Island in 1810 thirty-nine factories, in which were more than thirty thousand spindles.

Soon after 1806 a number of factories were built in various parts of Massachusetts.

February 27, 1807, an exemption from taxes for five years was granted by Act of the Legislature for a cotton mill, erected at Watertown by Seth Bemis and Jeduthan Fuller.

June 20, 1807, a factory was incorporated at Fitchburg.

March 12, 1808, the Norfolk Cotton Manufactory at Dedham was incorporated.

An association was formed January 1, 1811, for building a mill at Dorchester with two thousand spindles, and incorporated June 13, 1811, with a capital of $60,000.

February 23, 1813, an Act was passed to incorporate the Boston Manufacturing Company, better known as the Waltham Company, for the "purpose of manufacturing cotton, woollen, or linen goods." Instead of the customary designation of their place of business in the Act of incorporation, it authorizes them to conduct their business at Boston in the County of Suffolk, or within fifteen miles thereof, or at any other place or places, not exceeding four. Capital, $400,000.

The business was commenced in New Hampshire, as before stated, at New Ipswich in 1804.

The original proprietors of the first mill were Ephraim Hartwell, Charles Barrett, and Benjamin Champney.

In 1807 another mill was commenced upon the same stream, the Souhegan, by Seth Nason, Jesse Holton, and Samuel Batchelder, and put in operation in 1808. These were the first cotton mills built in the State of New Hampshire, and contained about five hundred spindles each. In 1805 the Legislature granted to the proprietors of the first mill an exemption from taxes for five years, and in 1808 the same exemption to the proprietors of the second mill.*

In December 1808, the Legislature of New Hamphire, by a general law, granted the same encouragement to those who should erect works for the manufacture of cotton, wool, salt, or glass. At the same session Acts were passed for the incorporation of the Peterborough Cotton Manufactory, and for the Exeter Cotton Manufactory. In 1809 were incorporated the second Peterborough Cotton Factory, and another in Chesterfield.

In 1810, one was incorporated in Milford, one in Swanzey, one in Cornish, one in Pembroke, and one at Amoskeag Falls.

In 1811, one at Walpole, one at Hillsborough, one at Meredith, and also a third at

* *History of New Ipswich*, pp. 224, 225.

Peterborough. Most of these mills went into operation within about a year from the time of their incorporation, so that at the commencement of the war with Great Britain, in 1812, there were, probably fifteen cotton mills in operation in New Hampshire, averaging not more than 500 spindles in each, or not more than six or seven thousand in all.

The first cotton mill in the State of Maine, then comprised in Massachusetts, was built at Brunswick in 1809, and soon after, another was erected at Gardiner.

Tench Coxe, in his report of the census of 1810, gives the number of cotton factories in New Hampshire at twelve, of which eight were in the County of Hillsborough.

The number given in other States was as follows: —

Massachusetts,	fifty-four.	Pennsylvania,	sixty-four.
Vermont,	one.	Delaware,	three.
Rhode Island,	twenty-eight.	Maryland,	eleven.
Connecticut,	fourteen.	Ohio,	two.
New York,	twenty-six.	Kentucky,	fifteen.
New Jersey,	four.	Tennessee,	four.

None in any other State.

All the factories built before the war of 1812 were built after the plan first introduced by Slater, with very little modification. His spinning was what was usually denominated the *water-frame*, built in separate sections of eight spindles each; but before 1808, when the second mill was built in New Hampshire, the spinning-frame, denominated the *throstle*, had been introduced and was adopted in this mill.

By this time the business had been commenced in a small way in several parts of New England, and the population were beginning to acquire some skill in the various operations of building machinery and its use. About 1807 and 1808, the embarrassments of commerce, the restrictions upon the importation of goods, and the consequent advance in prices, gave an impulse to the production of all such articles as could be manufactured here, to take the place of imported goods, particularly of cotton; and in 1812 there were said to be nearly forty cotton mills in Rhode Island, with about 30,000 spindles, and about thirty mills in Massachusetts within thirty miles of Providence, with about 18,000 spindles, amounting in the whole to 48,000 spindles.

The war with Great Britain in 1812 raised the price of goods to such extravagant rates, that articles of cotton, such as had been previously imported from England at seventeen to twenty cents per yard, were sold by the package at seventy-five cents.

This state of things stimulated the building of cotton factories to such a degree, that a list of the mills in and near Providence, including a number in Massachusetts at the close of the war, makes the number of mills 96, and of spindles 65,264, being an average of 680 spindles to a mill, eighteen of the whole number having less than 300 spindles each, and the largest, that of Almy, Brown, & Slater, 5,170 spindles.

A memorial to Congress, from the manufacturers of Providence in 1815, estimates * the number of mills within thirty miles of that town at 140, and the number of spindles at 130,000. But the most reliable statement of the extent of the business at that time is a list of the cotton mills in Rhode Island, and the adjoining parts of Massachusetts and Connecticut, lately communicated to the "Rhode Island Society for the Encouragement of Domestic Industry," by Samuel Green, Esq., of Woonsocket. It was compiled by a committee of manufacturers in 1815, for the purpose of making an assessment on each mill, to pay the expenses of sending an agent to Washington, to attend to the interests of the manufacturers at the approaching session of Congress, and bears the signature of John H. Clark, Secretary, James Burrill, Chairman, and Amasa Mason,

* This estimate is said to have been made under the direction of Mr. Burrill, a member of the Senate.

Philip Allen, and Samuel W. Green, Assessors. The number of mills and spindles given in

Rhode Island are:	mills,	99;	spindles,	68,142.
Massachusetts,	"	52;	"	39,468.
Connecticut,	"	14;	"	11,700.
Making in the whole,	"	165;	"	119,310.

A report of the Committee on Manufactures to Congress, in 1815, gives the following particulars of the cotton manufacture in the United States.

Capital,	$40,000,000	
Males employed of the age of 17 and upwards,	10,000	
Boys under seventeen,	24,000	
Women and female children,	66,000	
Wages of 100,000, averaging $1.50 per week,	$15,000,000	
Cotton manufactured, 90,000 bales, =	27,000,000	lbs.
Number of yards,	81,000,000	
Cost, averaging 30 cents per yard,	$24,300,000.	

When the importation of goods was recommenced at the close of the war, the sudden reduction of prices was destructive to all manufacturing operations. The business, that had been carried on during the war without much skill or economy, was prostrated, and the establishments that had been built up at an extravagant expense became worthless.

For the purpose of protecting this interest, which was supposed to have some claim upon the country on account of the aid afforded during the war, the tariff of 1816 was passed by Congress.

This measure was supported and advocated by Southern politicians, on the ground of encouraging the manufacture of our own cotton, instead of importing cotton goods from India, or those made from foreign cotton. On the contrary, it met with decided opposition from the people of the North, where navigation and commerce had been the favorite pursuits; and resuming their usual occupations and course of business, at the close of the war, they were disposed to look with an unfavorable eye upon the growth of a branch of business which it was supposed would interrupt the operations of foreign trade, and they were, of course, opposed to the tariff for the encouragement of manufactures;—but so much capital had been embarked in mills and machinery, and so many parties had become interested in their operation, that with the encouragement of the tariff great efforts were made to continue the business. Until this time the operation of cotton factories had been confined to the production of yarn, which was woven upon the hand-loom.

The power-loom had come into use to some extent in England previous to the commencement of the war of 1812.

The first attempt to weave by machinery was

made by M. De Gennes. His loom is described in the "Philosophical Transactions" in the year 1700. About 1765 a weaving factory driven by water, was built by Mr. Garside of Manchester. It was furnished with swivel looms, probably those invented by M. Vaucanson and described in the "*Encyclopedie Methodique.*" It was worked for a considerable time, but with no advantage, one man being required for each loom. (Guest, Hist. p. 44.)

Experiments had been made with various success, for several years, principally in Scotland, for the purpose of weaving by power. The power-loom, patented by Cartwright in 1785, was put in operation at Doncaster, but was unsuccessful. Another mill, with five hundred looms upon the same plan, was built at Manchester by Mr. Grimshaw in 1790, but was destroyed by a mob.

In Rees's Cyclopedia, article *Weaving*, is a very elaborate account of a loom invented by Mr. Austin of Glasgow, in 1789, and so far perfected in 1798, that it was put in operation at Mr. Monteith's mill, near Glasgow,—with what success does not appear.

A patent for a power-loom was taken by Miller in 1796, and another by Mr. Toad of Boulton in 1803. William Horrocks of Stockport took patents for a power-loom in 1803, and 1805, and for further improvements in 1813. This has now come into general use as the crank, or Scotch loom, and seems to have been the first that was put in operation with any success.

After the power-loom was so far perfected as to be capable of weaving, there was great delay in putting it in operation, for want of suitable machinery for dressing and preparing the warps. The great obstacle was, that it was necessary to stop the loom frequently, in order to dress the warp, as it unrolled from the beam, which operation required a man to be employed for each loom, so that there was no saving of expense.

To remedy this difficulty, Radcliff and Ross took patents, in 1804, for a dressing-machine, which to some extent supplied the deficiency.

Horrocks and Radcliff, sharing the common destiny of inventors, failed. This with other causes retarded the adoption of these machines, so that it is supposed that in 1813 there were not more than 100 dressers, and 2400 power-looms in use, in England and Scotland. Yet this was enough to alarm the hand-loom weavers, who, attributing to machinery the distress caused by the Orders in Council and the American war, made riotous opposition to all new machines, and broke the power-looms set up at

West Houghton, Middleton, and other places. (Baines, p. 235.)

From the time that the manufacture of cotton yarn began to be extended in this country, many attempts were made to construct machinery to weave by power. As early as 1806, a loom was built at Exeter, New Hampshire, by T. M. Mussey, which, as an experiment, would perform all the operations of weaving, but could not be called a labor-saving machine. Experiments were continued with great perseverance upon this loom until 1809, but I am not aware that the web, or the machine, was ever completed.

About the same time an attempt was also made at Dorchester. In this loom, the warp, instead of a horizontal, was in a perpendicular position, — in this respect resembling that patented by Johnson of Preston, England, in 1805, and that invented by Cartwright in 1785. I saw another in operation at Dedham in 1809, which was capable of weaving about twenty yards of coarse cloth per day, but none of these, though very ingenious experiments, were capable of being put in operation with such economy as to supersede the old process of hand-weaving.

During the few years of restriction upon importations, in 1809–10 and 11, and the war of 1812, such was the increased demand for any manufactures of cotton that could be produced by hand-looms, or by all the machinery then in operation for spinning, that little was thought of improvements or new inventions. This state of things continued in this country until the enterprise of Mr. Francis C. Lowell, Mr. Nathan Appleton, and their associates resulted in the successful establishment of the power-loom weaving at Waltham in 1814, of which such an interesting account has been given by Mr. Appleton in his "Introduction of the Power Loom, and Origin of Lowell," and also in the Memoir of Mr. Appleton, prepared for the Massachusetts Historical Society by Hon. Robert C. Winthrop.

The fact of the employment of the power-loom, successfully and extensively, in Great Britain was known in this country, but it was very difficult to obtain any accurate information upon the subject, and impossible to get any reliable knowledge of the construction of the loom on account of the restrictions upon the exportation of machinery, and the jealousy of communicating the plans of any of their manufacturing operations.

According to Mr. Appleton, (Introduction of the Power Loom,) the attention of Mr. Francis C. Lowell and himself was directed to this subject when they met in Edinburgh, in 1811, and Mr. Lowell determined, in accordance with Mr. Appleton's advice, to visit Manchester before his return to America, for the purpose of obtaining all possible information on the subject, with a view to the introduction of the improved manufacture in the United States. Mr. Lowell returned in 1813, bringing, without doubt, a better knowledge of the manufacturing operations of Great Britain than was possessed by any other person in this country, and which enabled him and his associates to establish the improved manufacturing system at Waltham, the incidents connected with which are detailed in the interesting pamphlet mentioned above.

Before 1810 it is supposed that power-looms were in successful operation in Scotland, as Mr. Lowell and Mr. Appleton mention them in their visit to Edinburgh in 1811, but in England it would seem they were more dilatory in adopting these improvements. An article in the "London Quarterly Review," published in 1825, says, with reference to the rapid increase of the town of Manchester, "At this moment there are upwards of thirty thousand looms worked by steam-engines. At the close of the year 1814 there was not one in use."

But the author of that article was under a

great mistake. "A factory for steam-looms was built at Manchester in 1806. Soon afterwards two others were erected at Stockport; and, about 1809, a fourth was completed at West Houghton. In 1818 there were at Manchester and the vicinity fourteen factories, containing about two thousand looms; and in 1821 thirty-two factories containing 5732 looms; and the number has been still further increased, so that there are at present (1823) not less than 10,000 steam-looms at work in Great Britain." (*History of the Cotton Manufacture, by Richard Guest.*) According to all the above statements, power-loom weaving had made but little progress in Great Britain before it was commenced in this country at Waltham.

Mr. Appleton's "Introduction of the Power-Loom" contains many interesting particulars of the steps taken in perfecting the machinery and organizing the various departments of the business. He relates the anecdote of a visit to Taunton to purchase the bobbin-winder, in substance the same as Mr. Moody related it to me. In the commencement of the business at Waltham, the filling, instead of being spun by the mule, as in England, was spun upon the warp-frame, and of course had to be wound upon a different bobbin to fit it for the shuttle. This, at first, was done by a machine invented by Stowell of Worcester; but Shepherd of Taunton had taken a patent for a machine for the purpose, which Mr. Moody thought preferable to the one they had in use; and he went with Mr. Lowell to Taunton to see if they could make an agreement for the use of their patent at a reasonable price. They found Mr. Shepherd disinclined to make any abatement, telling them that "they must of necessity come to his terms." Mr. Moody replied that, rather than give that price, he would invent a machine to *spin* the *filling* on a bobbin suitable for the shuttle. Mr. Lowell, who at once perceived the practicability of doing this, dropped the subject, and after some further conversation, took leave. After starting on their return, Mr. Lowell told Mr. Moody that he had suggested the plan of spinning the filling on the bobbin, and now he must accomplish it. Mr. Moody had made the observation only by way of chaffering for a bargain, but under these circumstances turned his attention to the subject, and the result was the invention of the filling-frame, which was patented and has continued in use ever since.

Mr. Moody also stated to me another incident respecting the construction and completing of the dressing-frame. At first they had used wooden rollers where the threads of the warp were submitted to the action of the size, but being constantly wet, the wood swelled and warped, so that the rolls would not fit accurately. They then tried covering the rollers with metal, by casting a coat of pewter on the outside; but after various methods of casting, sometimes in sand, and sometimes in a mould made of iron, for the purpose, they were still found to be imperfect. He at length thought of making a mould of soap-stone in which to cast them. Meeting his brother in Boston, who had been aware of the trouble he had experienced on the subject, he said to him, "*I think I shall get over the difficulty about the rollers, I intend to try soap-stone,*" meaning for a mould to cast them in. His brother replied, misapprehending him, "*Well, I should think soap-stone would make a very good roller.*" Mr. Moody made no reply, but took the hint, and made his rollers of soapstone, which has come into general use for the purpose.

In the power-looms that were first put in operation both at Waltham and Lowell, the motion of the lay, which beats up the weft, was given by weights. After a time, many objections were found to the use of weights, and it was thought expedient to give the motion directly from the revolving shaft by a cam. The mathematical calculations to give this cam such a form as would produce the accelerated velocity of a falling body, and thus to give the same motion as the weights, was a problem for Mr. Warren Colburn, whose skill in this and many other instances was made available in the application of mathematical science to practical mechanics.

After the interesting account given by Mr. Nathan Appleton, of the "Origin of Lowell," it is unnecessary to enlarge upon the subject. I recollect, however, a conversation in 1824, with Mr. Patrick Jackson, with reference to his expectations of the future prospects of the growth of Lowell, which at the time appeared to be extravagant and almost visionary. He stated that the purchases of real estate, at what was then East Chelmsford, on account of the manufacturing company, comprised about the same number of acres as the original peninsula of the City of Boston, before it began to be extended by filling up the flats, and said,—"If our business succeeds, as we have reason to expect, we shall have as large a population in the place in twenty years from this time, as there was in Boston twenty years ago." As extravagant as this prediction appeared at the time, when only two of the Merrimack mills were erected, and the population was less than 2000, it was more than realized.

Immediately after the power-loom was put

in operation at Waltham in 1814, measures were in progress for its introduction into Rhode Island, from a different source, and of a different construction.

William Gilmore emigrated to the British Provinces and came to Boston in September 1815. He had been acquainted with the power-loom and dressing-machine before he left Scotland. He brought to Boston certain small articles of Scotch manufacture, which in the state of trade at that time met a profitable market. Here he was met by Mr. Robert Rogerson, who was told that Gilmore had been employed in power-loom weaving, and understood the construction of the power-looms and dressing-machinery. Mr. Rogerson took him to Uxbridge and Smithfield, and made him known to John Slater. He proposed to Mr. Slater to build the machinery for power-loom weaving, — to have nothing for his labor unless he succeeded in putting the looms in operation. But the prospects of business at that time were so discouraging, that parties were not willing to enter into engagements, and he went to work as a machinist at Smithfield, where he commenced paying rent October 21, 1815.

Previous to this time a machinist by the name of Blydensburg had been employed at the Lyman Mills, in North Providence, in attempting to build a power-loom, but without success. Gilmore was employed, in the early part of 1816, to build twelve looms, and also machinery for warping and dressing, from the plans and drawings he had brought with him, which he accomplished to the satisfaction of his employer; and they were put in operation early in 1817. For the compensation of ten dollars he allowed Messrs. David Wilkinson & Co. the use of his patterns for building twelve other looms; and they got their twelve looms in operation nearly as soon as those built by Gilmore. This was the first introduction of the crank-loom in this country; and, to manifest their gratitude for the services rendered by Mr. Gilmore, the manufacturers subscribed to raise a fund of fifteen hundred dollars; and one of the subscribers to this fund refers to his receipt for payment of his subscription, which he has preserved, bearing date May 31, 1817,—thus showing the time when the crank-loom was put in operation in this country. The family of Gilmore, after his death, removed to Baltimore; and it ought not to be forgotten that one of his sons distinguished himself at the commencement of the present rebellion, by coming forward boldly among a disloyal people to supply, at his own expense, refreshments to one of the first regiments of soldiers from Rhode Island, which passed through that city soon after the assault upon the regiment from Massachusetts.

Gilmore's looms were built in a very substantial manner, so that some of them, after thirty or forty years use, still continue capable of doing very good work, after supplying some of the improvements since introduced, but without any important alteration in the mechanical construction of the loom. His warper and dressing-frame were such as were adopted in Scotland at an early period, but were much less perfect than those that had been invented at Waltham, and put in use there two or three years earlier.

Mule-spinning having been introduced in Rhode Island, the building of the power-loom, by Gilmore, completed the manufacturing system of that State within about three years from the time when the power-loom was put in operation at Waltham.

The inventions and improvements in the machinery at Waltham having been patented, including the loom, the double speeder, warper, dressing-frame, and filling-frame, and the right to the use of these patents being held at a high price, most of the mills already built in Rhode Island adopted the crank-loom, and introduced various plans in the process of making the roving, instead of using the patented speeder, among which was the tube-speeder, invented by Danforth, which was afterwards introduced to a considerable extent in Great Britain.

On the other hand, many of the mills, which had already been erected for spinning, in Massachusetts and New Hampshire, adopted the Waltham loom, and most of the large establishments, which were built from time to time in those States, followed the Waltham plan in regard to other machinery, as well as the loom.

There was thus established two different systems or *schools* of manufacturing, one of which might be denominated the *Rhode Island,* and the other the *Waltham* system.

One uses the live spindle, the other the dead spindle ; one, for filling, use the mule, the other the filling-frame ; one the Scotch dresser, the other the Waltham dresser ; one the crank-loom, the other the cam-loom. Both parties adhere pretty strongly to their own preferences, and manufacturers are still undecided which is the best in some particulars. It was not until ten years after the crank-loom had been in use in Rhode Island, that it was adopted at Waltham, or Lowell, and in neither place, nor in any of the mills that followed their system, was mule-spinning introduced until after 1830.

The machinery first constructed at Waltham was to a great extent the invention of ingenious machinists, who had no practical knowledge of manufacturing operations, and sometimes the facility of constructing the machine was more regarded than its adaptation to the use for which it was designed. The machinery introduced at Rhode Island, on the contrary, was adapted to its purpose by the skill acquired by practical experience in the English factories before the emigration of Slater.

But there was a difference in the general management of the business in the two systems, as well as in the machinery, and the establishment at Waltham formed a new era in the manufacturing business.

Mr. Slater had proceeded upon the English plan of employing families in the mill, often including children at an age when it would have been more proper for them to be at school. The consequence was the bringing together, in a factory village, a collection of families dependent entirely upon their labor, and often of parents who were disposed to live upon the labor of their children rather than upon their own, and exposed to suffering, as the operatives have been in England, whenever there was any interruption in the business. It was also the custom, instead of making payments in money, to establish what was called a Factory Store, from which the families were furnished with provisions and other articles, in payment for their labor, which resulted in a sort of dependence upon their employers.

At Waltham, they at once commenced the practice of the payment of wages in money, every week or fortnight, and also provided boarding-houses to accommodate all in their employ. This precluded the employment of children: as about half the usual wages of females would be required for the payment of board, the Company could not afford to pay board and wages to those who were not capable of doing full work. The result was that only those of mature age could find employment; and such usually having a home to which they could return in case of any interruption in the business, they were not subject to be left dependent or exposed to suffering.

From the time of the introduction of the power-loom, and the extension of its use, the cotton manufacture became established as an important element in American industry, particularly in New England. Under much discouragement at times by reason of the changing policy of the government as to the tariff of duties on imported goods, the number of spindles continued to increase. But we are not able to determine from the census reports the rate of increase with any certainty, as there was not, until the census of 1840, any specific statement of the number of spindles in the several States, or of the aggregate number in the United States.

In the Report of the census of 1840 the total number is stated at 2,285,337, of which 1,598,-198 were in New England. But in the census of 1850, neither the "Abstract" printed in 1853, nor the "Compendium" printed in 1854, or in the quarto Report, do we find any statement of the number of spindles, though there have been some statistics published that seem to imply that the returns of the marshals contained an enumeration of the spindles; but in the statements published by authority, the information as to the cotton manufacture is confined to the "Number of establishments," "Amount of capital," "Bales of cotton," "Tons of coal," "Value of materials," "Value of products," "Number of hands employed," and "Rate of wages," neither of which particulars afford so good an index of the extent of the business as the number of spindles; and the returns received, respecting most of these details, would only be an approximate estimate much less reliable than the number of spindles, which could be accurately counted.

The number of spindles in New England in 1850 was estimated upon reliable authority at 2,751,078;—the population of New England according to the census of 1850 was 2,728,106, making an average of 1008 spindles to 1000 inhabitants, which seems a very remarkable coincidence, and still more so when we find nearly the same proportion between the population and number of spindles in Great Britain at the same time as follows: —

In England, Scotland, and Wales, the population in 1850 was 20,793,552, and according to Ellison's Hand-Book the number of spindles was 20,857,062, equal to 1003 spindles to 1000 inhabitants; so that at that time we had become as much a manufacturing people in New England as they were in Great Britain. From 1850 to 1860 the population in New England had increased to 3,135,283. The number of spindles was reported at 3,959,297; looms, 103,204, being an average of about thirty-eight spindles to the loom.

By the preceding statements it would appear that the number of spindles from 1850 to 1860 had increased much faster than the population, so that in 1860 the number of spindles in New England would average 1265 to the thousand inhabitants.

The population of Great Britain, taken for April 8, 1861, was as follows: —

England and Wales, . . .	20,205,504
Scotland, ...	3,061,251
Making for Great Britain,	23,266,755

We have no reliable estimate of spindles in Great Britain at the above date; but at the same rate of increase per annum as between

1850 and 1856,—according to Ellison's Hand Book,—there is reason to suppose the number of spindles in 1861 could not be short of 33,000,000, which would be equal to an average of 1418 spindles to 1000 inhabitants. So that the spindles in Great Britain, as well as in New England, were increasing faster than the population.

In a lecture, delivered at Blackburn in 1857, by Alderman John Baynes, he says:—

"In 1846 there was no authentic or official statement of the number of spindles at work, and Messrs. DuFay & Co. of Manchester, at considerable expense, obtained much valuable information on this subject;" and the returns of the 'Factory Commissioners' show the number in 1850 and 1856, so that the account stands as follows:—

	DuFay & Co., 1846.	*Factory Commissioners.* 1850.	1856.
England and Wales,	15,554,619	19,173,969	25,818,576
Scotland,	1,729,878	1,683,093	2,041,139
Ireland,	215,503	119,955	150,502
	17,500,000	20,977,017	28,010,217
The estimate of Baynes for the rest of Europe and the United States is as follows:—	1846.		1856.
Europe,	7,585,000		14,650,000
United States,	2,500,000		3,950,000
Total,	27,585,000		46,610,217

He says further: "I have not been able to obtain any accurate data as to the number of spindles at present in operation in Europe or the United States, excepting one furnished by Mons. Bruno Henneberg, of Vienna, in reference to the extent of the cotton trade in Austria, viz: —

Lower Austria,	569,979
Upper Austria,	83,590
Styria,	25,464
Krain Gorr,	30,300
Tyrol,	214,094
Bohemia,	449,906
Lombardy,	129,046
Venice,	28,464
Hungary,	2,400
Total spindles,	1,533,243."

According to Gov. Woodberry's Report upon Cotton, the first cotton machinery introduced in France was in 1787, being about the same time with the first in operation in the United States. The first in Switzerland is stated on the same authority under date of 1798, and the first in Saxony in 1799.

In the statistics of Massachusetts, we have the most reliable account of the progress of the cotton manufacture in that State since 1837, made up from very careful returns from every town in the State: —

	Number of cotton mills.	Number of spindles.
1837	282	565,031
1845	302	817,483
1855	294	1,519,527
1860	301	1,688,471

By such data as we can obtain from the United States census, the whole number of spindles in the country, in 1840, was 2,285,337; 1860, 5,035,798.

The machinery for spinning cotton having been originally brought into use in England, was introduced into this country and France at about the same time, and at a later period into other countries of Europe. It was then quite imperfect, compared with what it is at present. Improvements have continued to be made both in this country and Europe; and many American inventions have been of sufficient importance to be adopted in Great Britain; and we have also availed ourselves of the improvements that have been made there, so that our best mills are not inferior, so far as machinery is concerned, to those of other countries. The rate of wages being higher here, we have had the greatest inducement to render our labor-saving machinery as perfect as possible.

Among the improvements in cotton machinery that have originated in this country, one of the most important is the combination of the train of three bevel wheels, to regulate the variable velocity requisite for winding the slender filaments of cotton on the bobbin of the roving frame, which was originally applied by a native of Rhode Island, Mr. Aza Arnold. This invention was successfully put in operation in 1822, and Mr. Arnold's patent was issued January 21, 1823. Previous to the use of this simple but admirably scientific adaptation of wheel-work to the roving frame, a very difficult arrangement of racks and pinions was used for the purpose, which had been introduced by Messrs. Cocker & Higgins of Manchester, which, though very ingenious, was attended with great cost for every alteration of the size of the roving for finer or coarser work. The roving frame, or double speeder, introduced at Waltham and Lowell, was subject to the same objection, which was the reason that most of the cotton mills in Massachusetts and New Hampshire, built after the Waltham plan, were generally adapted to the manufacture of a single article of sheeting or drilling, of the same number of yarn, without any means of changing from one fabric to another, according to the wants of the market.

The invention of Mr. Arnold, after having been used in the United States two years, was considered worthy of being introduced in England; and a model was taken to Manchester by an American in 1825; and in January, 1826, letters patent were obtained, for the same combination for the same purpose, by Henry Houldsworth, Jr.,—known as his *differential or equation box.* Ure, in his article on the cotton manufacture, after describing the apparatus for giving a uniform motion to the surface of the bobbins, while the circumference is gradually enlarged by the successive layers of the roving wound around it, and referring to the improvements patented by Houldsworth, says: "It may be considered the most ingeniously combined apparatus in the whole range of productive industry." It having been patented in England, Dr. Ure was not aware that it was an American invention, and gives the whole credit of it to his countryman, who also derived great profit from his patent,—while Mr. Arnold was hardly known by the public in his own country as the inventor, and, besides, spent most of the profits he had realized from the early sale of his patents in a protracted litigation to establish his rights, so that after the final judgment of the courts but little time remained for him to derive any income from his invention, and he acquired neither fame nor wealth by an improvement which has been of immense advantage to manufacturers, both at home and abroad.* It was not brought into use at Waltham or Lowell until two or three years after it was patented in England.†

Another American invention is the Danforth or cap spinner, which was invented in 1828 by Charles Danforth of Paterson, New Jersey, by whom it was patented in this country September 2, 1828. A patent was afterwards taken in the name of John Hutchinson of Liverpool, in 1830, when it went into extensive use, in England and other European States, for spinning the weft or filling, particularly before the late improvements in the self-acting mule.

George Danforth, of Massachusetts, was the inventor of the tube frame, otherwise known as the Taunton speeder, from its having been first built and brought into use in that place. This machine has likewise been used to a considerable extent in England, being a much less

* This differential or equation box, thus applied to cotton machinery, is probably the same said to have been first invented in France by Pecqueux in 1813, and constructed by Perrelet in 1823, to regulate the movements of an orrery. — See "*Bulletin de la Societé pour l'encouragement de l'industrie nationale,*" 1823.

† For the particulars in relation to this improvement, I am indebted to a communication from Mr. Zachariah Allen, being an extract from a manuscript work he is preparing respecting the cotton manufacture, and which it is hoped he will not further delay giving to the public.

expensive machine than what is called the double speeder or fly frame, and answering very well for the purpose in the manufacture of coarse yarn. It was patented in England, by Mr. Dyer of Manchester, in 1825, having been in use in this country, and patented September 2, 1824.

A very cheap machine for making roving, called the eclipse speeder, and capable of very rapid operation, was invented by Gilbert Brewster of Poughkeepsie, New York, and patented April 18, 1829. It was used for a time to a considerable extent on account of the cheapness of the machine and the great quantity of work produced. It was introduced into Manchester in 1835, and built by Sharp, Roberts & Co., and known as the eclipse roving-frame.

The plate speeder was likewise brought into use in Manchester in 1835, by Mr. Neil Snodgrass, who imported one from America.

What is called the stop-motion on the drawing frame was designed and brought into use at Saco, Maine, by the writer, in the year 1832. Before this invention, the slender fleeces of cotton from the card, not having received any twist to give them strength, and with hardly tenacity enough to support their own weight in the operations of the drawing-frame, where four strands or more were combined into one, required constant watching, lest the deficiency of one strand, by breaking or any other cause, should render the work imperfect; and, with the greatest care, it was impossible to prevent many accidental imperfections. By the introduction of this improvement, not only was much loss of time prevented in stopping the machine to correct mistakes, but the speed might be increased with safety, and with the assurance that the work was correctly done. No patent was taken for it in this country, the importance of it not having been duly appreciated by the inventor until it had been put in use by other parties; but a patent was afterwards taken by H. Houldsworth in England, from which the inventor derived some profit; and no machinery is now built without adopting this improvement, either in England or this country.

Mr. Montgomery, in his work on the "Cotton Manufacture of Great Britain and America," considers the application of the stop-motion on the warper, which was first used at Waltham, an important improvement over the warper used in Great Britain, which requires the utmost attention to notice instantly when a thread breaks; and when this happens, the end of a broken thread may wind around the beam so far as to require some minutes to find it and put the machine in motion again;—but this cannot happen with the American warper, which stops instantly when a single thread breaks. This application of the drop-wire to stop the machine is said to have been suggested by Jacob Perkins, well known for many ingenious inventions.

Of the dressing machine invented at Waltham, Mr. Montgomery says: It is much more simple, more easily attended and kept in order, besides requiring less power and oil, than any he has seen, either in England or Scotland, and can be made for about half the cost of those used in Manchester and Glasgow. He says that those which, instead of the measuring roller, are mounted with steam-drying cylinders, invented and patented by Samuel Batchelder in 1835, produce the greatest quantity of work.

A spinning-frame called the ring-spinner was invented by John Sharp, of Providence, about 1831, and, with some later improvements, has come into extensive use in this country, and is supposed by many to produce yarn cheaper than any other machine, but its use in England to any great extent has probably been prevented by the great improvements in the self-acting mule.

For a long time after the power loom went into operation in Great Britain, the use of the old hand-temples was continued for keeping the cloth extended to the width of the warp in the reed; and the changing of these temples, as the weaving proceeded, required the watchful care of the weaver, and was often neglected.

The use of the self-acting temples, invented by Ira Draper, of Weston, Mass., and patented January 7, 1816, was introduced at Waltham about 1825, and, it is believed, long before anything of the kind was used in England.

A correspondent says he never saw a self-acting temple in use in Scotland, his last visit there having been in 1855. In 1850 one was pointed out to him in England as a novelty, so that it must have been many years after the general use of this important invention in this country before it was adopted in Great Britain. Mr. Montgomery says, of the weaving by power in America, the self-acting temples, besides saving a great deal of labor on the part of the attendant, make a very superior and uniform selvedge, and expresses his surprise that they have not been more generally adopted in Great Britain.*

* What renders this still more surprising is, that, as early as 1805, in an English patent to Thomas Johnson and James Kay,

Many other American improvements of minor importance might be enumerated.

The use of leather belts instead of iron gearing for transmitting motion to the main shafting of a mill, was introduced by Mr. Paul Moody, at Lowell, in 1828. Though not to be called an invention, this proved to be a very important improvement, and was entirely original in its application to the transmission of fifty or an hundred horse-power by a single belt, and has been very generally adopted in the mills in New England.

Of similar character was a Dynamometer, not specifically applied to the cotton manufacture, but affording better means of ascertaining the power for driving machinery, either by water or steam than any instrument which had been used for the purpose. This was designed and built at Saco by the writer, and exhibited at the Fair of the Mechanics' Institute in Boston in 1839, when a medal was awarded for the invention.

It was made known in Europe by a description in a work of J. Montgomery on the Cotton Manufacture, published at Glasgow in 1840; and in a German periodical* is a long article upon

among other improvements in the loom is included a revolving temple.

* Dingler's *Polytechnic Journal*, Vol. 84, p. 7.

the various dynamometers in use, in which this is included as taken from the "Proceedings of the Society for the Promotion of Industry in Prussia," and is distinguished in the engraving as "Batchelder's dynamometer," and described as simple and preferable to any known apparatus for ascertaining the power actually used in driving machinery.

In regard to manufacturing skill, so far as relates to carding and spinning, in which they have had in Great Britain the experience of one generation before we began, they must be farther advanced than we are, particularly as they serve a regular apprenticeship to the business, and follow the same employment through life; while with us, so far as regards the female operatives, and to a certain extent as to others, it is only an employment for a few years, until an establishment or the cares of a family require their attention; and boys or men seldom follow the business long enough to acquire any skill, before they return to some agricultural employment; so that the greater part of those at work in our mills are only a succession of learners, who leave the business as soon as they begin to acquire some skill and experience; and therefore, in relation to carding and spinning, the English manufacturers are far in advance of us. In regard to weaving, the power-loom having been in use here nearly as long as in Great Britain, their manufacturers have not so much the advantage of us, as a large proportion of our weavers have had some experience in hand-loom weaving before commencing in the factory. But there is a difference in our management in regard to weaving, which has an effect. With us a weaver generally attends four looms, sometimes more, and the looms operate at such a moderate speed, and are so organized with self-acting temples and otherwise, as to enable the weaver to do this with ease. In England there is a prejudice, and perhaps a stronger influence, against attending more than two looms, and it is attempted to make up for this by extraordinary speed.

Four looms, at a speed of 120, would weave 480 threads per minute; two looms, at an increased speed of fifty per cent., would weave only 360 threads, so that a weaver would produce only three quarters as much cloth. In an establishment in England of 630 looms, of which I have had an opportunity to examine all the particulars, and compare them with a mill here, weaving a similar article, I find no weaver, out of the whole number of 346, attending more than two looms, and, comparing the price paid for weaving, I find the cost to be at least fifteen per cent. more than in this country; and the wages even at this rate were such as induced the weavers to strike for additional pay.

The advantage of manufacturing in England, on account of wages, is much less than we have generally supposed. The business is, no doubt, conducted there more economically in many particulars than with us. The cost of machinery is less, and the interest on capital less, and fine articles, or such as require experience and skill, can undoubtedly be produced cheaper there than here; but it is questionable whether heavy goods, such as drilling and sheeting, which make up a very large proportion of the consumption of this country, can be produced cheaper than in the United States.

One of the countervailing advantages in this country, compared with the expense of manufacturing in Great Britain, is the abundance and cheapness of water-power. There was, some time ago, an attempt, by interested parties, to prove that steam-power was cheaper than water-power. Facts afford a practical refutation of this theory. In England, where coal and steam-power is much cheaper than in most of the manufacturing districts of this country, there are many instances where water-wheels, and all the necessary arrangements for the use of water-power, are provided at great expense, where water-power can be used used for only half the year.*

In this country, at Manayunk, where the canal for the supply of coal to the city of Philadelphia passes by the walls of the mills, and where steam-power can be produced at less cost than in any other manufacturing section of the country, the mills are driven by water-power at an annual rent equal to sixty dollars per horse-power, or about four times the cost of water-power at Lowell or Lawrence, on the Merrimack River, where the rent and interest at six per cent., payable on the cost of water-power and land for a mill, will average a fraction over fifteen dollars per horse-power per annum.

Mr. Montgomery, in his comparison of "Cotton Manufacture in Great Britain and the United States," estimates the cost of steam-

* Mr. Zachariah Allen says: "Notwithstanding the abundance of coal in England, and the very general use of the steam-engine, water-power is highly valued in all the manufacturing districts, and mills are erected on streams, which in many instances are sufficient to turn the water-wheels, and operate the machinery during only a part of the year." And in his visit to Stanley Mills, he mentions "five large cast-iron water-wheels," and says, "My surprise was greatly excited on being informed, that, with all these water-wheels, a deficiency of water rendered it necessary to keep a steam-engine in operation three or four months of the year."

power in Massachusetts at about ninety dollars a year per horse-power, which he says is about double the cost of the same power in Glasgow. There is much uncertainty in all estimates of the cost of steam-power, arising in part from the want of accuracy in the admeasurement of the power of steam-engines, and an over-estimate of their power, as well as from other causes.

The cost of steam-power has been much reduced by improvements in the steam-engine within a few years, both here and in Great Britain; but if we reduce the above estimates by one half, it would leave the cost of steam-power at $22.50 in Scotland, which would be fifty per cent. above the cost of water-power on the Merrimack.

If we take the improvements in the Corliss engine, which is said to have reduced the average consumption of coal to two and a half pounds to the horse-power per hour, the cost of fuel only, with coal at $6 per ton, would be $27.90 per annum, or nearly double the cost of water-power on the Merrimack,—besides the wages of engineer and fireman, and also subject to fluctuations in the price of coal according to the market, which at present would be fifty per cent. above the estimate.

This estimate of water-power, at $15 per

horse-power per annum, also includes the cost of land suitable for mill-sites at Lowell and Lawrence, the two principal manufacturing cities in the country; but such is the superabundance of water-power in New England, and other parts of the country, that it could be obtained, in situations favorable for manufacturing, for half the cost above stated.

According to present appearances, the history of the *introduction* of the cotton manufacture may almost be considered a history *completed.* There are at this time probably not much more than one third the number of spindles in operation that there were in 1860.

In the Report of the Boston Board of Trade, for the year 1863, Mr. Edward Atkinson states that he made a list of the principal mills in the New England States and New York, to ascertain how many of the spindles were stopped in June, 1862, and found the number to be 2,327,000; and again, November 1st, made a similar estimate, and found the number to be 2,169,650. According to the census of 1860, the number of spindles in those States was 4,288,113, so that in June and November, 1862, there were only about one half of the spindles in operation, and since that time the number has been considerably reduced; and Mr. Atkinson estimates that the total number in operation, December 31st, was about 1,700,000, which would be about two fifths of the number in those States.

We have no means of estimating, with any accuracy, the diminished operations in Great Britain, but, from the complaints of distress for want of employment, there is reason to suppose the interruption of the business there, has not been less than in this country. A confirmation of this opinion may be found in the Report of the "Cotton Supply Association," of April 1, 1863, according to which the total importation of cotton into Great Britain in 1862 was only 4,678,180 cwts., while the total importation for the year 1859–60, before any interruption to the business, was, according to Mann's "Cotton Trade of Great Britain," 10,946,331 cwts.; so that the supply for 1862 was but little more than four tenths of the former importation. Of this reduced supply, instead of the usual proportion of 85 per cent. of American cotton, the proportion is reduced to $4\frac{1}{4}$ per cent. of American, including all that has been received from the West India islands and other places concerned in running cotton from the blockaded ports.

While the supply from America has been thus diminished, an increase has taken place from other countries as follows:—

	1861. *cwts.*	1862. *cwts.*	*Increase. cwts.*
Greece, ...	415	1,865	1,450
Turkish dominions, . .	633	41,212	40,579
Egypt, ...	365,108	526,897	161,789
Western coast of Africa,	1,389	3,380	1,991
Mauritius, ...	7,288	17,688	10,400
Madras, ...	175,682	335,432	159,750
Bengal, ...	462	92,292	91,830
New Grenada, . .	1,383	10,342	8,959
Brazil, ...	154,378	208,384	54,006
China, ...		14,695	14,695
	706,738	1,252,187	
Total increase,			545,449

The stimulus of high prices has probably occasioned a still further increase of production in those countries for the present year; and this, together with the cultivation of cotton in other climates favorable to its production, with the advantage of the employment of free labor, will probably have the effect, within a few years, to supply the world with cotton of an improved quality, without dependence upon slavery, or any monopoly of the Southern States.

As to the production of cotton in this country for the year or two past, we have no means of forming an estimate, except by conjecture. However, when we consider the diminished number of slaves employed in the South, and the interruption to the cultivation of cotton from other causes, and the increased proportion of labor necessarily diverted to the production of grain and provisions, we may be satisfied that the power of King Cotton has suffered as much in the field as in the factory.

The events of the last two years have produced such an entire change in the cultivation of cotton, and its manufacture, both in this country and abroad, that it is difficult to form any opinion as to the future, and yet it would be intensely interesting to be able to look forward a few years in anticipation of coming events. Much will depend upon the supply and price of cotton. The cost to New England manufacturers for each month from January 1861 to September 1863, taking the average of the market from the highest to the lowest price of the month, has been as follows:—

	1861.	1862.	1863.
January . .	12¾	34½	73
February . .	12½	23½	89
March . .	12¼	26½	72
April . . .	13	28¾	64
May . . .	13	28½	61
June . . .	15	30½	52½
July . . .	15¾	41	63
August . . .	17	48½	66½
September . .	20	54½	73
October . .	23	58	
November . .	23¼	63½	
December . .	31½	68	

The proprietors of those mills, which have been in operation for the year past, have found their purchases of middling cotton to average rather above than below sixty cents per pound, which is about five times the price for the few years preceding. At this rate the quantity of goods that could be manufactured and sold at a moderate profit, has kept in operation about one third of the spindles in the Northern States.

It is evident that the wants of the community will continue to require a considerable supply of cotton manufactures, notwithstanding the high price of the raw material, and if there should be such an increase in the supply as to produce a decline in price, the demand for consumption would increase, but such an increase in the supply must be very slow and uncertain.

The imports of cotton into Great Britain in 1862, above the quantity imported in 1861 from all those countries from which there had been any increase, was about seventy-seven per cent. upon the quantity imported from the same countries in the former year, or nearly five per cent. on the whole imports, — and though the stimulus of high prices may produce a still further increase from many foreign sources, the supply from such sources must be quite limited, when we consider that only one sixth part of the cotton manufactured in England has been derived from all other countries than the United States, — and where the increase depends upon new planting, it will require a long time to make it available; so that the principal reliance must be on resuming the cultivation in this country under more favorable circumstances than the present.

With reference to the operations of our cotton mills, we shall undoubtedly import less and manufacture more of our textile fabrics than we have been accustomed to do, and whenever business shall resume its ordinary course, it will require a large quantity of goods, not only to supply the consumption, but to fill up the deficient stock in all the channels of trade, — goods may therefore be expected to maintain their price according to the cost of the raw material.

But all these calculations as to results can only be considered as *probabilities*, subject to be interfered with in the present unsettled state of affairs, by so many contingencies from political as well as other causes, that the changes and chances for a few years to come may be as strange and unexpected as have been those of the few years past.

SOME PARTICULARS IN RELATION TO COTTON AND COTTON MANUFACTURES,

CHRONOLOGICALLY ARRANGED.

The earliest patent granted in Great Britain for any important improvement in manufacturing, was that to John Kay, for the invention of the Fly-shuttle, May 26, ······· 1733

The first machinery for spinning, of which we have any satisfactory account, was that invented by John Wyatt, soon after 1730, and which was patented in the name of Lewis Paul, June 24, ······· 1738

A patent for carding machinery, in which is described the cylinder card, as first used by hand, was granted to Lewis Paul, August 30, ······· 1748

A second patent for spinning machinery was granted to Lewis Paul, June 29, ······· 1758

The invention of the drop-box by Robert Kay, by means of which filling of different colors could be used with the fly-shuttle, ······· 1760

According to Guest, the spinning-jenny was invented by Thomas Highs, ······· 1764

The invention is also claimed by James Hargraves, who took a patent for it, June 12, ······· 1770

Arkwright's first patent for spinning machinery, July 3, 1769

Act of Parliament to prohibit the exportation of machinery, ······· 1774

Second patent to Arkwright, including Carding, Drawing, and Spinning, was granted December 16, ······· 1775

Patent to Robert Peele, for carding, roving, and spinning, February 18, ······· 1779

Mule-spinning invented by Samuel Crompton (not patented), ······· 1779

James Watt took his first patents for improvements in steam-engine, March 12, ······· 1782

Subsequent patents in 1784 and 1785.

Power-loom invented by Edmund Cartwright, first patent, April 4, ... 1785

Subsequent patents 1786, 1787, 1788.

Arkwright's patents declared void, ... 1785

Cylinder printing was patented by Thomas Bell, July 17, 1783, and introduced in Lancashire................ 1785

Bleaching by oxymuriatic acid was discovered in France by Berthollet,.................................... 1785

And introduced at Manchester practically,* 1788

Legislature of Massachusetts made a grant to Robert and Alexander Barr, to aid them in building machinery for spinning cotton,................................ 1786

First machinery for spinning cotton put in operation in France,.................................... 1787

Grant to Thomas Somers by the Legislature of Massachusetts, to aid him in completing machines for spinning, 1787

First cotton factory built in the United States at Beverly, Massachusetts, ... 1787

Some spinning-jennies were put in operation in Philadelphia and Providence,........................... 1788

Commencement of the cultivation of Sea Island cotton in Georgia, from Pernambuco seed, ... 1789

Samuel Slater came to this country, and was employed at New York, where he said they had in operation one carding engine and two spinning-jennies, at the close of the year 1789

Slater came to Providence, Rhode Island, and began building a cotton factory, ... 1790

In which they commenced spinning early in.......... 1791

Cotton gin invented by Eli Whitney in 1793, and patented March 14,................................ 1794

Cotton mill built by Slater and others at Pawtucket, Massachusetts, ... 1798

First cotton mill and machinery in Switzerland,....... 1798

First spinning machinery in Saxony, ... 1799

Water-mill at Beverly, Massachusetts, with Arkwright machinery, ... 1802

* See Note C.

* First cotton mill in New Hampshire commenced at New Ipswich in 1803, and went into operation.......... 1804

Second mill at Pawtucket, Massachusetts, ... 1805

Mill at Pomfret, Connecticut, ... 1806

After the patents for a power-loom to Edmund Cartwright, several other patents were taken by other parties, some of which went into partial operation, but none with any success, until the invention of the dressing-frame by Radcliff and Ross, with the assistance of Thomas Johnson. Guest gives the date of this invention 1803; Baines in 1804. One of the patents to Thomas Johnson was issued February 28, 1803, and another June 2, 1804; and a mill for weaving was built at Manchester in 1806, which may be considered the date of the successful commencement of power-loom weaving, ... 1806

Mill built at Smithfield, Rhode Island, by John Slater, 1807

Mill built at Watertown, Massachusetts,.............. 1807

Second cotton mill in New Hampshire at New Ipswich, 1808

Norfolk cotton factory at Dedham, incorporated, ... 1808

First cotton mill in Maine, at Brunswick, ... 1809

Mill at Dorchester, Massachusetts, incorporated, ... 1811

Incorporation of Boston Manufacturing Company, known as *Waltham Company*,.............................. 1813

Power-looms in operation at Waltham, being the first in the United States,.................................. 1814

William Gilmore emigrated to this country, ... 1815

And put the crank-loom in operation in Rhode Island, .. 1817

First cotton factory built at Lowell, ... 1822

Self-acting mule patented by Richard Roberts, March 29, 1825

First cotton mill at Lawrence, Massachusetts,......... 1849

There is so much uncertainty and inaccuracy as to the dates of many improvements and inventions in cotton machinery in the accounts given by Guest, Kennedy, Baines, and others, who seem to have copied one another's errors, instead of correcting them, that I have referred for the dates of all patented improvements to the collection of "*Specifications of Inventions from March* 2, 1617, *to October* 1, 1852," in Great Britain, contained in one hundred and sixty volumes of text, and three hundred and ten volumes of plates, a copy of which may be found in the Boston Library.

* See Note D.

NOTES.

NOTE A.

This early patent for spinning by machinery deserves particular attention for various reasons. In the first place, for the accuracy with which it describes the process of roller spinning; and secondly, because it did not go into successful operation for thirty years, when Arkwright took his first patent; and thirdly, because the existence of this patent was entirely unknown at the time of the trials on the validity of Arkwright's patents, in 1781 and 1785, when the attempt was made to show that Arkwright was not the original inventor; and even afterwards, in 1828, at the time of the controversy between Guest and the "Edinburgh Review," in which the experiments of Thomas Highs, about the year 1764, were attempted to be set up as the original of the Arkwright machinery.

This invention was made soon after 1730, by John Wyatt, and was patented in the name of Lewis Paul, June 24, 1738. The process, in substance, is thus described in the specification. The wool or cotton being prepared, one end of the roping is put between a pair of rollers, which being turned round, by their motion draw in the cotton to be spun, and a succession of other rollers, moving proportionally faster than the first, draw the roving into any degree of fineness which may be required.

A second process is then described that is quite unintelligible without drawings. — The specification then proceeds to describe a *third* process as follows: "In some other cases only the first pair of rollers is used, and then the bobbins on which the yarn is spun, are so contrived as to draw faster than the rollers give, and in such *proportion as the first sliver* is *proposed to be diminished.*"

Though the first process described in Paul's patent coincides exactly with Arkwright's roller spinning, it does not appear to have been put in operation even by the inventor. The third process only was used, as appears by the letter of Charles Wyatt, who says, — "the wool had been carded in the common way, and was passed between two cylinders, from whence the bobbins drew it by means of the twist," — and also by the patent taken for an improvement twenty years after the first, June 29, 1758, which, after describing the preparation of the rove, says, — "which being put between *a pair* of rollers, is by their turning round, delivered to the *nose of a spindle*, in such proportion to the thread made as is proper for the particular occasion." The spindle is so contrived as to *draw faster than the rollers give*, in proportion to the length of yarn, into which the matter to be spun is proposed to be drawn.

From this it plainly appears that the extension of the roving to produce the yarn did not take place by the different motion of successive pairs of rollers, but by the stretch between the rollers and the spindle, somewhat similar to the drawing of the roving while receiving the twist, as on the spinning jenny or the one thread wheel.

There are no drawings in existence to explain the processes in this first patent, but the specification and engravings (published in Baines' History of the Cotton Manufacture, p. 139) of the second patent to Paul in 1758, for improvements in the machinery then in use, show plainly that they relate only to the third process of the first patent, and would be very imperfect compared with the process of roller spinning, if that had then been brought into use.

Mr. Kennedy (Baines, p. 125,) from an examination of specimens of yarn furnished by Mr. Wyatt's son, pronounced "that it could not be said by competent judges that it was spun by a similar machine to that of Arkwright."

It may seem very strange that so many years elapsed after the invention by Wyatt of the true process of roller spinning, before it was put in operation by Arkwright in 1769, notwithstanding the intervening attempt to construct machinery for the purpose by Highs, and perhaps by others; for the means of supplying yarn for the weavers, seems to have been an object which engaged attention very extensively. The reason, however, that none of these plans for spinning went into successful operation probably was the defect in the preliminary processes.

We see no mention of *drawing*, or any operation between the card and the spinning. A manufacturer will appreciate the importance of this operation, and others also, when they are told that in some of our mills for fine spinning, (that at Portsmouth for instance,) the drawing and doubling is carried to the extent that the sliver as it comes from the card is doubled more than two thousand times, so that each thread as it is spun consists of so many ends of carding extended and drawn down to the size of the yarn.

These operations tend to straighten the fibres of the cotton and lay them parallel, so as to give strength in the operation of spinning, and also to the yarn after it is spun, and it may be doubtful now, whether the most perfect Arkwright spinning machinery would operate successfully with roving produced without this preliminary process, or made according to the specification in the second patent to Paul in 1758, which says, the cotton to be spun "must first be carded upon a card made up of a number of parallel cards with intervening spaces between each, and the matter so carded must be taken off each card separately. The several roves or filliaments so taken off must be connected into one entire roll, which being put between a pair of rollers," etc.

It was not until the first patent by Arkwright that any patent was granted for *drawing machinery*, or that the process of drawing received due attention, and this in all probability was what insured his success.

Baines, p. 182, says, "The drawing and roving frames depend on exactly the same principles as the spinning frame, for which Arkwright took out his patent of 1769; — they were modifications of that machine, but the new processes, which they were made to perform were indispensable to the perfecting of the yarn. He was the first to introduce the drawing process and to apply the spinning rollers to the purpose of roving.

In the yarn examined by Mr. Kennedy, the difference in the position of the fibres in that spun on Wyatt's machine from the parallelism of those in the yarn spun by Arkwright, was probably what enabled him to pronounce that the former had been spun by a different process.

NOTE B.

The first patent to Edmund Cartwright for a power-loom was granted April 14, 1785, and he also took further patents for improvements in 1786–87 and 88, which seem to comprise all the necessary movements for weaving by power, including the stop-motion for the shuttle, and self-acting temples. He built a mill for weaving at Doncaster, which was unsuccessful.

About 1790, Mr. Grimshaw of Manchester, under a license from Mr. Cartwright, erected a weaving factory, operated by steam, which after various difficulties was burnt, and Guest says, "for many years no further attempts were made in Lancashire to weave by steam."

Guest says Mr. Austen of Glasgow invented a loom in 1789, which was further improved in 1798, and a building for two hundred looms was erected by Mr. Monteith in 1800. No patent is recorded for such a loom to Mr. Austen. Baines says Mr. Monteith built such a mill in 1801 for two hundred looms, invented by Robert Miller, whose patent was granted June 28, 1796.

In 1803, April 14, a patent was taken by John Todd for a loom in which the lay was operated by a crank, and with a shuttle stop-motion.

In 1803, April 20, a patent was granted to William Horrocks, and another, May 14, 1805, but both relate to the motion of the shuttle, and neither comprise the essential requisites for a power-loom. Baines says Horrock's loom is the one that has now come into general use. This must of course refer to his loom, as improved, by the patent granted to him July 31, 1813, in which the lay is driven by a crank.

In 1805, August 9, a patent was granted to Thomas Johnson and John Kay, for a loom with revolving temples, and such a let-off motion as is still in use; and in 1806, August 1, to Peter Marsland, for a loom which operated with a crank.

Several of these looms seem to have been complete in all that was necessary for power-loom weaving; but though some of them actually went into operation, none of them were capable of superseding the old process of weaving by hand. This was probably not so much, from any defect in the machinery, as for want of the suitable preparation of the web, and it was not until the invention of the dressing-frame by Thomas Johnson, one of whose patents bears date February 28, 1803, and the other June 2, 1804, that power-loom weaving could be considered as successfully established. In this case, as in relation to the spinning machinery, it was a long time after the true principles were discovered, and the machinery invented, before the practical skill was acquired to put it in operation.

Guest says a factory for steam-looms was built at Manchester in 1806, and soon afterwards two others at Stockport, and about 1809 a fourth was completed at West Houghton.

It does not appear which among the foregoing patent looms was first put in use, but according to Baines, we may conclude that the loom of Horrocks, after his improvements in 1813 was adopted, so that it would appear that power-looms were not completed and in successful operation for any considerable time before their introduction at Waltham in 1814, and it should be recollected that as late as 1813, mobs were breaking the power-looms in the neighborhood of Manchester, and among others, those above mentioned at West Houghton.

NOTE C.

According to Baines, it occurred to Berthollet that cloth might be bleached by chlorine, formerly termed oxymuriatic acid, and in 1785, having tested it by experiment, he made known the discovery. James Watt learned this from Berthollet at Paris, and on his return to England, late in 1786, he introduced the practice at the bleach-field of his father-in-law, Macgregor, near Glasgow. After this, without any knowledge of Watt's experiments, but acting upon the suggestion of Berthollet's papers, Thomas Henry of Manchester, who was delivering lectures on dyeing, printing, and bleaching, pursued his experiments on the subject and made known the result to the Manchester bleachers, in 1788, by a public exhibition of the bleaching of half a yard of calico.

NOTE D.

In a periodical published at Manchester a few years ago, a claim was set up that the first cotton mill in New Hampshire was built at Amoskeag Falls in 1804. This claim was supported by the testimony of Jonas Harvey, the owner of a saw-mill, who says he leased the privilege to Benjamin Prichard in the fall of 1804, when the cotton mill was built. This seemed to make a very strong case. But it was within my knowledge that the first acquaintance of Prichard with the cotton business was by means of his employment in the first factory which went into operation in New Ipswich in 1804, and also that he was employed in building the second factory in New Ipswich, which was commenced in 1807, and of course there must have been a mistake in the date when he built the mill at Manchester. Accordingly, I find on referring to the records of New Ipswich, that he did not leave that place until 1807, and continued to pay a poll tax there until that date. Besides, I was a petitioner to the legislature of New Hampshire in 1808, for exemption from taxes for the second mill in New Ipswich, and during the progress of the act for that purpose through both branches of the legislature there was no suggestion of there being any other cotton mill in the State at that time, except the two at New Ipswich. The large manufacturing establishments at Amoskeag Falls in Manchester were commenced in 1831.

www.ingramcontent.com/pod-product-compliance
Lightning Source LLC
LaVergne TN
LVHW021427110826
845150LV00007B/2115

* 9 7 8 1 4 2 5 5 0 7 6 2 6 *